# CAPACITY BUILDING FOR LOCAL BODY LEADERS

**By the same Author**

— New Panchayati Raj System at Work : An Evaluation

— Grassroot Democracy in Indian Society

— Dynamics of New Panchayatiraj System in India (10 Volumes)

---

**About the Author**

**Ganapathy Palanithurai,** Professor in Rajiv Gandhi Chair, Gandhigram Rural Institute is an academic activist working with the people in rural areas for building the capacity of the leaders and people to reinvent sustainable grassroots democracy. He is heading the Department of Political Science and Development Administration, in Gandhigram Rural University, Tamil Nadu. His policy advocacy role at the governmental level is increasingly felt at present in all the three levels, namely, sub-regional, regional and national as he does more field work than theorization. He has been associating himself with State Planning Commission of Tamil Nadu, Population Foundation of India, Rajiv Gandhi Foundation, CAPART, Ministry of Rural Areas and Employment and DANIDA (Danish-Indo Development Agency) in specific areas of activities in connection with empowerment of people. He is in the network of the Non-Governmental Organisations for Panchayat activities. He involves himself in capacity building exercise for local body leaders. He has evolved training module and manual for local body leaders. He has to his credit twenty-four books, seventy-five articles in reputed journals, ten working papers, seven monographs, seven review articles on three major areas, namely, Legislative Behaviour, Ethnicity and Panchayati Raj System. He was a recipient of Fellowship from Śastri Indo-Canadian Institute, New Delhi and World Academy of Art and Science, USA. He has visited the US and Canada, on academic assignments. He was a visiting fellow in the MiGill University, Canada in 1989. He is a life member of Indian Institute of Public Administration, Indian Association of Public Administration, Indian Association of Political Science, Indian Association of American Studies, and Indian Association of Canadian Studies. He is a member of the expert committee constituted by the Government of Tamil Nadu, to monitor the training programme for local body leaders.

# CAPACITY BUILDING FOR LOCAL BODY LEADERS

**G. PALANITHURAI**
Professor and Head,
Department of Political Science and Development Administration
Gandhigram Rural Institute — Deemed University
Gandhigram-624 302
Tamil Nadu

**CONCEPT PUBLISHING COMPANY, NEW DELHI-110059**

ISBN 81-7022-888-3

First Published 2001



*Published and Printed by*
Ashok Kumar Mittal
**Concept Publishing Company**
A/15-16, Commercial Block, Mohan Garden,
NEW DELHI-110059 (India)

*Phone* : 5649024, 5648039
*Fax* : 091-11-5648053
*E-mail* : publishing@conceptpub.com

*TO*
*THE DIVINE MOTHER*

# FOREWORD

New Panchayati Raj came into being as a system of governance since 1992. It is a new addition to the institutions of governance (Central and State Governments) and it gives a new dimension to the federal polity and administration. The rejuvenation of grassroot institutions has numerous problems as the workload and responsibilities of these institutions are heavy and onerous. To take up these tremendous responsibilities, the leaders of the Local Bodies have to be capacitated. Enhancing the capacity of the leaders is the vital need of the hour.

The Department of Political Science and Development Administration, Gandhigram Rural Institute had taken initiative to create awareness among the people from various parts of Tamil Nadu about the New Panchayati Raj System since 1992. It has produced abundance of reading materials for the Panchayat leaders. Awareness generation programme had been carried out for four years with the support of non-governmental organisations. The Department has created a network of NGOs for the purpose of creating awareness among the people. Further, it conducted a series of workshops to review the 73rd Constitutional Amendment Act and made certain recommendations to modify the same. Through the network of NGOs pressure had been mounted on the Government to enact a suitable legislation in accordance with the provisions of the 73rd Constitutional Amendment Act.

After the enactment of the Tamil Nadu Panchayati Act 1994, a workshop was organised to review the Tamil Nadu Panchayati Act of 1994 and a wide range of suggestions had been given to modify the existing Act. Many of the recommendations, published in the form of a book, have been accepted by the Government of Tamil Nadu. By recognising the activities and services of the Department of Political Science and Development Administration the Rajiv Gandhi Foundation came forward to create a 'Chair' specifically for conducting studies on the Panchayati Raj System. After the creation of the Chair a number of studies have been carried out and an array of books and articles have been published. The

Government of Tamil Nadu have given the responsibility of preparing training modules to the Rajiv Gandhi Chair.

Tamil Nadu Government have recognised the Rajiv Gandhi Chair for Panchayati Raj Studies as a nodal centre for training. After the election to Local Bodies, the Rajiv Gandhi Chair for Panchayati Raj Studies has been entrusted with the task of conducting leadership training for the women leaders of Urban Local Bodies of Tamil Nadu. The Chair has covered sixteen districts. Population Foundation of India has asked the Chair to evolve a training module for training on Social Development and test the same in two districts of Tamil Nadu. The Chair has conducted training programmes in two districts.

The Department of Political Science has been associating itself with the State Planning Commission of Tamil Nadu for the preparation of Ninth Five Year Plan document especially for Panchayati Raj. CAPART (Council for Advancement of People Action and Rural Technology) has given the responsibility of offering training programme to Gram Panchayati leaders in seven districts. DANIDA (Danish-Indo Development Agency) has given the responsibility of conducting training programmes for Gram Panchayat Presidents and Vice-Presidents on Water Supply and Sanitation. Thus, the Rajiv Gandhi Chair has organised training programme extensively for local body leaders.

Besides the training programmes, it has organised several Conferences, Seminars and Symposia on varied themes akin to Panchayati Raj. All the programmes have been documented properly. The training programmes have opened the eyes of the leaders and administrators. The documents which have been prepared from the training programmes carry several messages and they highlight the ills of the local bodies too. These documents have the course module and contain the experience of the leaders who have undergone the training. For exchanging the experience it has been decided to bring the documents into a book form.

All the activities are done by a dedicated team in the Department of Political Science and Development Administration under the dynamic leadership of Dr. G. Palanithurai. He is assisted by Mr. V. Ragupathy, Mr. M. A. Thirunavukkarasu, Mr. M. Gurusamy, Mr. S. Devaraj and Mr. A. Thangathurai. All the members are to be appreciated. The Gandhigram Rural Institute is proud of the laurels brought by the Department of Political Science and Development Administration through its historic contributions in strengthening the Panchayati Raj Institution. I wholeheartedly appreciate the effort taken by Dr. G. Palanithurai in organising the training programme and documenting the whole exercise. Further, I appreciate the effort taken by the Concept Publishing Company to publish the documents. I express my sincere thanks to the funding agencies like Government of Tamil Nadu, CAPART, DANIDA and Population Foundation of India for their generous financial support in organising the training programmes.

**Dr. N. Markandan**
*Vice-Chancellor*
*Gandhigram Rural Institute — Deemed University*
*Gandhigram - 624 302.*

## TRAINING TEAM

| | | |
|---|---|---|
| *Coordinator* | : | Dr. G. Palanithurai |
| *Deputy Coordinator* | : | V. Ragupathy |
| *Master Trainers* | : | M. A. Thirunavukkarasu<br>M. Gurusamy<br>S. Devaraj<br>A. Thangathurai |

# PREFACE

After the enactment of the 73rd Amendment to the Constitution of India, several steps have been taken to put the institutions in proper tract in proper form to get the maximum output from the grassroot level institutions. Yet the institutions are struggling as conflicting perceptions are persisting among the functionaries and leaders about the role of New Panchayati Raj Institution in the society. Hence, it is imperative that capacity building exercise is offered to all sections from top level bureaucracy to the bottom level leaders.

In Tamil Nadu no serious effort was made to popularise the concept among the leaders and the people after enactment. It was argued that the new system can function effectively only when the basic objectives of the amendment are known to all concerned. All of a sudden election was declared and candidates contested in the election. Results have been declared and yet confusion persisted over the role and responsibilities of the elected leaders and the functionaries in the new system in a new context. Time and again Gandhigram Rural Institute and especially the Department of Political Science and Development Administration appealed to the government at the provincial level to conduct the capacity building exercise for the Panchayati leaders. Yet due attention was not given in this regard owing to different reasons.

But officials at their level convene meetings of local body leaders and brief them about the activities to be carried out in the rural areas with their involvement. Officials considered their briefing to Panchayat leaders as training. As a result the leaders are trained to carry out the assignments given to them by the State and Central Governments. For the past three years the leaders have been oriented to carry out the schemes and programmes of the governments both at the Centre and the State. The Government of Tamil Nadu especially the Secretary of Municipal Administration Ms. Malathi, I.A.S., has felt that the women leaders of urban local bodies should be sensitised and hence, she has entrusted the responsibility of conducting one-day orientation programme for the women leaders of urban local bodies to the Rajiv Gandhi Chair for Panchayati Raj

Studies, Gandhigram Rural Institute. Thus, the Rajiv Gandhi Chair has conducted training programme for women leaders of sixteen districts in Tamil Nadu. But with regard to rural local bodies, no systematic effort was made by the concerned Department. The National Institute of Rural Development conducts programme and invite rural local body leaders for interaction. This type of sporadic interaction will not enhance the capacity of the leaders and change the perception, behaviour and performance of the representatives of the people. Having given several proposals to the Government of Tamil Nadu for initiating training for local body leaders, the Gandhigram Rural Institute has been recognised as a nodal centre for training and yet financial assistance was not provided.

The Rajiv Gandhi Chair for Pancyhayati Raj Studies has submitted a proposal to CAPART (Council for Advancement of People Action and Rural Technology) for conducting training for local body leaders. CAPART has provided financial assistance to conduct the capacity building exercise for Gram Panchayat Presidents of five districts.

To train the Gram Panchayat Presidents a training manual was prepared and training was given to them at a limited level. While the training team was in the programme, the Population Foundation of India has come forward to evolve a strategy to achieve Social Development through Panchayats and a training programme was prepared for this purpose. Based on the strategy training was conducted for local body leaders of two districts, namely, Dharmapuri and Dindigul. It was conducted successfully. While we are in the last leg of the training DANIDA (Danish-Indo Development Agency) has insisted that Gandhigram should take up the responsibility of conducting training for local body leaders in Cuddalore and Villupuram districts as DANIDA operates water supply and sanitation programme in both the districts. Even, for this programme we have developed a training module and based on the training module, we have conducted the training programme in two districts.

The Social Welfare Board of Tamil Nadu under the chairmanship of Ms. Geetha Viswanathan requested the Rajiv Gandhi Chair to associate itself with the Board in the training programme organised for women Gram Panchayat Presidents in five districts. The Rajiv Gandhi Chair has conducted the training programme for women leaders of Gram Panchayats.

The Population Foundation of India has entrusted another programme to the Rajiv Gandhi Chair to develop model Panchayats in the district of Dindigul for replication. For this project an interface training programme was conducted. The selected ten Gram Panchayat Presidents have been taken to Kerala State and made to interact with the Gram Panchayat

Presidents of Kerala and see the activities of the Panchayats. Thus, the Rajiv Gandhi Chair conducted several training programmes both in the campus and outside. It associated, itself with various organisations to conduct the training programme. From the training programme, reports have been prepared based on the experience in the field. All the reports are compiled in this small volume for the benefit of other organisations and researchers.

It is prepared with the assistance of the training team, namely, M.A. Thirunavukkarasu, M. Gurusamy, S. Devaraj and A. Thangathurai. They have conducted the training programmes and reported their experience to the coordinator. As coordinator of the programme, I have documented all the details. Though I have given guidance, the team has carried out the works to the fullest satisfaction of the trainees and the sponsoring organisation. I have to thank the trainers for their commendable work.

Likewise, I should express my sincere thanks to the funding agencies like DANIDA, CAPART, Social Welfare Board, Tamil Nadu Institute of Urban Studies, Population Foundation of India for their liberal contribution for this exercise without whose support we could not have done this job.

For our task there are various individuals and institutions involved and to them I express my profound gratitude. Last but not the least, my colleagues and my family members who have allowed me to perform this work without any disturbance by doing their role and function perfectly deserve my sincere thanks.

Gandhigram G. PALANITHURAI
20-08-1999

## CONTENTS

# 1

# TRAINING PROGRAMME CONDUCTED FOR GRAM PANCHAYAT PRESIDENTS*

73rd Constitutional Amendment Act and the subsequent enactment of the State Local Bodies Act of 1994 provide a large number of responsibilities to the local body leaders. To discharge all those responsibilities in highly fragmented communities and complicated administrative system the local body leaders need adequate skill and capacity. Of all the prerequisites for smooth functioning of local bodies to deliver goods, capacity building exercise for local body leaders is foremost and imperative. It has been indicated in many fora that the leaders or respresentatives recruited for different authoritative bodies, namely, national parliament and State legislature should have adequate skill and capacity to perform their role and function in a fast changing socio-political and economic system and therefore, their training is an imperative need. But nobody took keen interest in it. As a consequence our parliamentary institutions are fastly deteriorating in their standard of performance. The local body institutions cannot and should not follow the beaten path of the higher level representative institutions as these bodies are closely monitored by the people and the representatives in the local bodies are to face the people every day and they should be so responsive to their calls. Hence a programme of training for Gram Panchayat Presidents was conceived by Rajiv Gandhi Chair for Panchayati Raj Studies and the proposal was sent to CAPART Hyderabad for financial support. As Rajiv Gandhi Chair for Panchayati Raj Studies was instrumental in evolving a training module based on the exercise done at the national level in Hyderabad for Tamil Nadu Planning Commission, CAPART, Hyderabad was kind enough to

* Sponsored by CAPART.

approve the module and sanction the required financial support to take up the training programme for Gram Panchayat leaders for about five districts. To start with, the exercise has been planned for Gram Panchayat Presidents in two districts, namely, Dindigul and Sivagangai and on experimental basis the same exercise has to be done for women and *dalits* in three districts, namely, Madurai, Ramanathapuram and Pudukkottai. In the first leg the evolved training module can be tested and accordingly modifications could be effected in the training. This programme was a beginning of a massive exercise. It is being done in batches. Each group consists of forty to forty-five presidents of Gram Panchayats. The training content of the programme includes the historical aspects of the Panchayati Raj System, constitutional aspects of the Panchayats, main provisions of the federal and state Acts, planning experience in India for economic growth and development, micro-level planning for comprehensive development of the areas, activity dimensions of the Panchayats on twenty-nine subjects in 11th Schedule, behavioural and performance dimensions of the presidents of the Gram Panchayats. The training lays more emphasis on dialogue and discussion. Vital issues have been video-taped and shown to them. Field trips have been arranged to model panchayats to demonstrate the success of programmes by the active involvement of the people. Pre- and post-evaluation of the training programme has been done through administering an interview schedule. Information has been collected from the leaders on the practical problems faced by them when they perform their role and function in the Panchayats.

**Perception of the Leaders on New Panchayati Raj System**

Before the commencement of the training exercise a schedule is being circulated among the trainees to elicit their perception and understanding of the New Panchayati Raj System. Their perceptions are explained here.

The perception that Panchayats are to perform service function is lingering in the minds of leaders as they are not aware of the provisions and main implications of the New Panchayati Raj System. They had a rough idea about the new system that it would fulfil the basic needs of the people and provide basic amenities to the community. They presumed that more powers would be given to Panchayats and equally more amount of money would also be given to panchayats. This impression has been created among the people by the media. They said that they did not find copies of the 73rd Amendment to the Constitution of India and hence they could not read the provisions of the Act. They did not care to read the provisions of the Tamil Nadu Panchayati Act of 1994 even though it was supplied to the Gram Panchayat leaders as the entire Act is in a language which is not understandable to them despite the fact that it is in Tamil. Even the candidates who have contested in the election, did not believe that the election would be conducted when the Act was enacted. Likewise they had a notion that the political parties will not evince interest in conducting the election. The moment election was announced, they entered the fray with the hope of enjoying more powers and resources as MPs and MLAs. They have openly admitted that they have spent money for electioneering ranges between rupees thirty-five thousand to two lakhs.

In the pretest schedule, there are about twelve questions. They are:

(a) Basic objectives of the New Panchayati Raj System;
(b) Special features of the new system;
(c) Functions of the New Panchayati Raj System;
(d) Responsibilities of the Presidents of Gram Panchayats;
(e) Ways and means to perform their role successfully;
(f) Methodology of organising the people and to involve them in the development process;
(g) Possibilities for rural economic development;
(h) People's participation in panchayat activities;
(i) Women's development;
(j) SC/ST development activities;
(k) Social justice; and
(l) The characteristics of a good leader in the panchayat.

Their responses to the above questions are as follows :

(a) Panchayat is to elicit their basic needs;
(b) Panchayat is to fulfil the basic needs;
(c) Panchayat is to implement the Government schemes for the poor;
(d) Panchayat is to provide basic facilities in the rural areas;
(e) Panchayat has three-tier Panchayat system;
(f) Panchayat will be a permanent entity;
(g) Panchayat will have 29 subjects in 11th Schedule;
(h) Panchayat will have a Gram Sabha;
(i) Panchayat is to select beneficiaries for government schemes;
(j) Panchayat is to supervise fair price shop;
(k) Panchayat is to mobilise resources for Panchayats;

(l) Panchayat is to construct culverts, bridges, houses for the poor;
(m) Panchayat is to lay roads, and dig wells;
(n) Panchayat is to maintain sanitation;
(o) Panchayat is to protect the environment;
(p) Panchayat is to do afforestation activities;
(q) Panchayat is to protect the common property resources;
(r) Panchayat is to take steps for women's development;
(s) Panchayat is to convene the panchayat meetings periodically; and
(t) Panchayat is to organise Gram Sabha meetings periodically.

The presidents of Gram Panchayats are having a rough idea, about what the new Panchayats have to. They again and again reiterate the service function as the function of the Panchayats. They forget about the original function of the local bodies as per the provisions of the Act. They are not well aware of the basic objective of the 73rd Constitutional amendment. They have not mentioned about the economic development activities and social justice. During the past one and half years, the Gram Panchayat presidents have been oriented by the officials in implementing schemes and programmes of the federal and State governments. Hence, their mindset is that the Gram Panchayat leaders are to implement schemes and programmes of the governments. Even in discussion they ask more questions about schemes. They are not much worried about the planning, and resource mobilisation for economic activities.

**Problems the Gram Panchayat Presidents face in the Field**

Group discussions are being arranged to elicit their problems which they face in the field while performing their role and function. Their problems are presented here :

1. Presidents of Gram Panchayats are not aware of all the rural development programmes and schemes. They know only a few programmes from the officials.
2. Needs of the people are going on increasing which need enormous amount of resources. To meet all their requirements there is no plan.
3. Employees and teachers working under the purview of Panchayats are not employees of Panchayats and they are all employees of the Government and hence, the employees are not accountable to local bodies; as a result schools are not properly managed. Yet the presidents are to set right the primary schools

in the villages.

4. Resources (both in the form of money mobilised from within and drawn from Panchayat union and DRDA for schemes) are inadequate to meet the demands.
5. Capacity of the workers working in the rural areas is inadequate to meet the problems in the rural society. Not attending the repair work of street lights or motors fixed in overhead tanks in time and the technicians causing inordinate delay. Rates for the repairing work are very low and hence nobody turns towards these works. For the purchase of materials for the repairing work or replacement, presidents have no option but to give more money than the market rate.
6. Providing shelter is a major problem in the rural areas. Whether, it is providing *patta* or getting housing scheme, presidents have to face a plethora of problems as needs are more and available resources are limited. Moreover, while providing these facilities discretion of officials plays an important role rather than the rules of the programmes and schemes.
7. Integrated Rural Development Programme (IRDP) beneficiary selection is a major problem due to the interference of the politicians, MLAs and MPs.
8. Getting the village map from the revenue department is very difficult. There is absolutely no cooperation from the department in this regard.
9. It is very difficult to remove encroachment from the common properties. It requires the support of revenue department and police, which is not available to the Gram Panchayats.
10. Common property resources have not been maintained well to yield income to Panchayats since they are not under the control of the local bodies.
11. Needs are unmet even after the Panchayats came into being.
12. No relationship between the needs and the schemes.
13. Still we have complicated administrative procedures at the lower level.
14. Difficult to provide employment opportunities to the needy.
15. Officials domination over the elected leaders is evident and they dictate terms to the leaders.
16. People's mindset is that everything has to be done by the government. People are only to receive. They expect each and everything to be taken care of by the local body leaders.

17. Common property resource management should be given to local bodies. Sand, quarry and other natural resources are the properties of the community. But now on a single order they are taken away from the people without getting the consent of the community.
18. Powers of the Union Engineer are unlimited and UE is the embodiment of corruption. He is more powerful than the Block Development Officer. He is the person responsible for clearing bills, proposals and hence, he makes the Gram Panchayat presidents to dance to his tune. Union Engineer demands 15 per cent commission for each and every work.
19. Interference of MPs and MLAs in the affairs of local bodies is excessive and their words are respected and their interference in the local body affairs disturb the activities of the local bodies. Increasing the amount for MLAs and MPs would attempt to kill the local bodies.
20. In all government functions organised in the rural areas, the concerned constituency MP and MLA are invited but the local body leaders are not respected and invited.
21. Presidents are elected by the people and vice-presidents of Gram Panchayats are elected by ward members. But so far as the cheques are concerned, the vice-president has also to sign them. It disturbs the atmosphere and administration.
22. Women presidents are not respected by the officials. Sometimes they were ill-treated in the offices. They face lot of problems in the offices of the government.
23. More flexibility in the schemes should be allowed to local body leaders to meet the basic needs of the people.
24. Public distribution system should be supervised by the Panchayats in the local areas.
25. Government orders are not properly circulated among the local body leaders.
26. For each and every transaction officials in the Panchayat union demand money openly.
27. There is no linkage between the Panchayats and the cooperatives.
28. Makkal Nala Paniyalargal are in the Panchayats and they have to work under Panchayats and get their salary from Panchayats. Yet, in practice they are not working in coordination with the president. Hence, the procedure of giving salary to them in Panchayat union office should be stopped.
29. Ration cards are to be distributed through Gram Sabha to eliminate

bogus cards.

30. For making estimate and settlement of bills, officials take lot of time but to execute the programmes and schemes officials give short time to leaders. This has to be avoided.
31. Birth certificate, death certificate, community certificate should be issued by the Panchayats through resolution. Erring leaders have to be punished.
32. There is no linkage between the revenue department and the development department.
33. The role of district Panchayat is not known to Gram Panchayat presidents.
34. MPs, MLAs, District Panchayat Members, Block Panchayat Members are operating funds to execute certain works in the villages without the knowledge of the people and the Gram Panchayats. All these works are to be integrated. At present these works were not based on need and hence lot of money is being wasted by allotting them for construction work.
35. Panchayats are advised to take up works without claiming any advance. Where do they find money for work. Even, after completing the work, the presidents have to move from pillar to post to get the money from the offices and for which they have to give bribe to officials at all levels.
36. Allocation of money to MP, MLA, District Panchayat Member, Block Panchayat Member tempted the Village Panchayat Ward Members to demand that they should also be given some amount of money for works.

**Their Perception after the Training**

Before the valedictory session, again an interview schedule is being distributed to elicit their opinion about the implications of training. Apart from filling up the schedule, they openly express their opinion about the training programme in the valedictory session. Some VIP will be there in each programme to distribute the certificate. This valedictory session has an advantage for the trainers to correct themselves in their methodology of the training. Their perceptions about the Panchayati Raj after the training programme have been compiled and presented below :

1. They perceived the long-term implications of the New Panchayati Raj system.

2. The mindset that local bodies are to execute schemes and programmes of the governments has been changed and the new mindset that local bodies are to work for economic development and social justice has been created.
3. They learnt to make the Panchayats as people's Panchayats and not the government's Panchayats.
4. It is not power but it is only responsibility that makes the Panchayats as a self-governing institution.
5. They realise that without money Panchayats can do many programmes in the villages.
6. They realise the original functions of the local bodies.
7. They feel that they are change agents.
8. Key provisions of the 73rd Constitutional Amendment Act and Tamil Nadu Panchayati Raj Act are known to the Gram Panchayat presidents.
9. How to prepare perspective plan for rural development is known to them.
10. It is recognised as a governing institution.
11. Schemes and programmes of the government are known to them.
12. Role and responsibilities of the presidents are known to them.
13. How to create employment opportunities in the villages by making use of the available skills is known to them.
14. How to mobilise resources in the rural areas is known to them.
15. How to make the Panchayats as movement of the people is known to them.
16. How to get the government orders from the officials is known to them.
17. How to get the works done in the government offices is known to them.
18. How to conduct the Panchayat administration in a transparent way is known to them.
19. How to mobilise people and to involve them in the Panchayat activities are known to them.
20. Issues and solutions are known to them.
21. How to protect the environment is known to them.
22. How to make the rural areas Green is known to them.

***Trainers***

Dr. G. Palanithurai — Professor in Rajiv Gandhi Chair<br>GRI, Gandhigram.

| | | |
|---|---|---|
| Dr. S. Ponnuraj | — | Dean, Faculty of Sanitation, GRI, Gandhigram. |
| Dr. N. Narayanasamy | — | Professor in Extension Education, GRI, Gandhigram. |
| Dr. N. Meenakshi Sundaram | — | Reader in Rural Industries and Management, GRI, Gandhigram. |
| Dr. K. P. Vasantha Devi | — | Reader in Home Science, GRI, Gandhigram. |
| Dr. S. Narayanasamy | — | Reader in Gandhian Thought and Peace Science, GRI, Gandhigram. |
| Dr. V. Ragupathy | — | Reader in Political Science, GRI, Gandhigram. |
| Sri A. Udaya Kumar | — | Training Associate, KVK, GRI, Gandhigram. |
| Sri M. A. Thirunavukkarasu | — | Research Associate, Rajiv Gandhi Chair, GRI, Gandhigram. |
| Sri A. Thangathurai | — | Research Associate, Rajiv Gandhi Chair, GRI, Gandhigram. |
| Sri M. Gurusamy | — | Research Associate, Rajiv Gandhi Chair, GRI, Gandhigram. |
| Sri S. Devaraj | — | Research Associate, Rajiv Gandhi Chair, GRI, Gandhigram. |
| Sri E. Vellaichamy | — | Director, CHERU (NGO) — Vadamadurai. |

***Associated by***

| | | |
|---|---|---|
| Mr. K. Tamilarasan | — | Research Officer, ICSSR Project, Dept. of Political Science, GRI. |

Mr. G. Umashankar — Research Associate,
Population Foundation of India,
Dept. of Political Science, GRI.

*Secretarial Assistance*

Mrs. Radha Manickam
Sri P. Rajendran

*Material Supplied to them*

1. A printed book of 400 pages
   with details of 73rd Constitutional Amendment Act;
   with details of the Tamil Nadu Local Bodies Act of 1994;
   with a brief history of Panchayati Raj;
   with a brief outline of Planning Experience in India;
   Micro-level Planning and participative development process;
   All schemes and programmes of the Centre and State Governments with all details;
   Resource mobilisation;
   Common Property Resource Management;
   MPs area development programme details;
   Importance and implications of community action;
   MLAs constituency development programme details; and
   the hurdles to make panchayats as self-governing institution
2. All government orders pertinent to local bodies
3. A well-designed jute bag
4. A scribbling pad
5. A pen
6. Important address of institutions to get more information about Panchayat activities

*Course Module*

| | | | |
|---|---|---|---|
| 1. | Number of Trainees | : | 30 |
| 2. | Duration | : | 5 days |
| 3. | Institution | : | Rajiv Gandhi Chair for Panchayati Raj Studies, Gandhigram Rural Institute |
| 4. | Whether Residential | : | Yes |

**Daily Schedule**

| | | |
|---|---|---|
| • Lecture Sessions | : | 9.30-12.30 |
| • Lunch | : | 12.30-14.30 |
| • Discussion Sessions | : | 14.30-16.00 |
| • Field Visit | : | 16.00-19.00 |
| • Dinner | : | 19.00-20.00 |

**Course Contents**

*General Orientation*

(a) Plan process in the country
(b) Democratic Decentralisation
(c) Rural Development Programmes.

*Subject Orientation*

(a) Panchayati Raj : Concept and Status
(b) Salient Features of Panchayati Raj structure in the concerned State Gram Sabha, Village Panchayat, Panchayat Union and District Panchayat
(c) Functions of Panchayat Union with particular reference to
    (i) Planning and Implementation of district level plans
    (ii) Management of rural development schemes and
    (iii) Monitoring and Evaluation
(d) Resource of Panchayat Union
(e) Role and responsibilities of Staff of Panchayat Union
(f) Supervision and Control over Panchayat Unions and Village Panchayats

*Role Orientation/Behavioural Aspects*

(a) Role and Responsibilities of Elected Representatives at village level
(b) Role and Responsibilities of Officials at village level
(c) Relationship between Officials and Elected Representatives
(d) Collective leadership and people's participation
(e) Experience sharing
(f) Team work

*Activity Orientation*

1. Agriculture, including agricultural extension
2. Land improvement, implementation of land reforms, land consolidation and soil conservation
3. Minor irrigation, water management and watershed development
4. Animal husbandry, dairying and poultry
5. Fisheries
6. Social forestry and farm forestry
7. Minor forest produce
8. Small-scale industries, including food processing industries
9. Khadi, village and cottage industries
10. Rural housing
11. Drinking water
12. Fuel and fodder
13. Roads, culverts, bridges, ferries, waterways and other means of communication
14. Rural electrification, including distribution of electricity
15. Non-conventional energy sources
16. Poverty alleviation programme
17. Education, including primary and secondary schools
18. Technical training and vocational education
19. Adult and non-formal education
20. Libraries
21. Cultural activities
22. Markets and fairs
23. Health and sanitation, including hospitals, primary health centres and dispensaries
24. Family welfare
25. Women and child development
26. Social welfare, including welfare of the handicapped and mentally retarded
27. Welfare of the weaker sections, and in particular, of the Scheduled Castes and the Scheduled Tribes
28. Public Distribution System
29. Maintenance of community assets

*Management Orientation*

(a) Administrative management of programmes in Panchayat Unions

(b) Emerging role of Panchayats in Planning and Development
(c) Maintenance of records
(d) Preparation of village plans
(e) Implementation of Special Programmes
(f) Panchayat Fund and Budget
(g) Maintenance of accounts
(h) Audit and Accounts
(i) Resource Mobilisation
(j) Conduct of Business
  (1) Meeting of Gram Sabha
  (2) Meeting of Panchayat
  (3) Preparation of Agenda
  (4) Quorum
  (5) Vote of No-Confidence
  (6) Disqualification of Members
  (7) Minutes of Meeting
(k) State Government agencies operating at State/District/Block level
(l) Agencies operating within District such as Banks/Cooperative/ Voluntary Organisation
(m) Protection of community lands
(n) Management of primary schools

*Field Orientation*

Visits to some successful institutions, demonstration farms, programmes. The objective is essentially educative and to expose the trainees to successful projects. Visits may be arranged to model Panchayats and to knowledgeable individuals, social workers in nearby areas, or to a cooperative bank.

(A) *Illustrative List of Institutions/Organisations/Projects*

(1) A Successful Panchayat
(2) A Successful Cooperative Society
(3) Farmers' Mandal, Mahila Mandal
(4) A Cooperative Bank
(5) Agriculture Research Farm/Seed Multiplication Farm
(6) Dairy Farm, Cattle and Poultry Farms
(7) Afforestation Programme
(8) Cottage and Village Industries Centres etc.

(B) *Projects*

(1) An Irrigation or Hydel Project
(2) A Key industry
(3) A Model Housing Colony

(C) *Individuals*

(1) A successful farmer
(2) A successful cattle breeder and poultry breeder
(3) An Anganwadi Worker

**Conclusion**

The capacity building exercise for Gram Panchayat presidents has to go a long way to achieve its results. It is a good beginning by which their mindset has been changed. Lot of information has been exchanged. Their potentiality has been drawn out. 60% of attendance has been ensured despite the instruction from the government. Material supplied to them is properly used by the participants of the training programme. Women are more enthusiastic than men. One aspect is obvious from their interactions i.e. they need a supporting base as government is not favourable to them.

# 2

# TRAINING PROGRAMME CONDUCTED FOR GRAM PANCHAYAT PRESIDENTS AND VICE-PRESIDENTS ON WATER SUPPLY AND SANITATION*

**Preliminary Exercise**

To begin with the resource persons were oriented about the training methodology with special reference to Water Supply and Sanitation for two days on 23rd and 24th of January, 1999 at the Project Management Group (PMG) Office, Cuddalore. The contents of the orientation programme included objectives of the proposed training programme, the level of trainees, methods to be adopted and the material to be used in the training programme. The resource persons were taken to a few villages where the DANIDA schemes are being carried out effectively at present to familiarise them with this scheme. As soon as the orientation to the resource persons was over, the resource persons started preparing the training material. Preview was done at Gandhigram itself.

**Signficance of the Training Programme**

The aim of DANIDA is to implement its Water and Sanitation Scheme only through the village Panchayat and more particularly to involve the people generally and the women specifically in all aspects of the project, namely, Planning, Implementation, Monitoring and Maintenance. As representatives of the people, the village Panchayat presidents and vice-presidents have a major role to perform in implementing the schemes and

* Sponsored by DANIDA-I

programmes of the Central and State Governments and for which the leaders are to be oriented about the scheme so that they can take the message to the people, convince and motivate them to use this opportunity to reap the maximum benefits of the scheme. It was also felt that as these Panchayat presidents and vice-presidents enjoy goodwill of the people, they can influence the people to become the beneficiaries of the scheme. The capacity of the presidents and vice-presidents of the Gram Panchayats, to perform their role and responsibility has to be enhanced and this has been the basic objective of this programme. Hence, the training programme is imperative and essential.

### President and Vice-President

In the present arrangement, both president and vice-president are made to function as single entity. The joint responsibility of both has to be explained to them in such a fashion as to evoke positive response from the leaders. This arrangement is to overcome the problem of conflict between the president and vice-president of the Gram Panchayats in Tamil Nadu.

### Logistics Arrangements

The DANIDA had made elaborate logistics arrangements like providing training materials, lunch and refreshment to the trainees, accommodation for the training staff and hall for the training programme. These were carried out meticulously with utmost care. More particularly, the training venues were comfortable and it created a conducive atmosphere for learning. During the evening, the women participants who had ventured to come from a long distance and remote villages were taken by DANIDA van to their respective villages which propelled them to come for the second day training also.

In the training programme the DANIDA has arranged an exhibition with specimens of hand-pumps, tool kits etc. Also posters with pictures illustrating training modules, estimation for various types of latrines, water schemes were also exhibited which attracted the participants very much. In the course of training programme, video programmes were also taken up, covering the training sessions. The training sessions were photographed.

### Training Schedule

The training was conducted in 15 batches. Each programme was for a duration of two days. The details of dates and venues as well as attendance are given below :

**Attendance Statement**

| Batch | Total Strength | | | No. of Participants | | | |
|---|---|---|---|---|---|---|---|
| No. | President | Vice-President | Total | President | Vice-President | Total | %age |
| I | 17 | 6 | 23 | 15 (88.20) | 6 (100.00) | 21 | 91.30 |
| II | 16 | 25 | 41 | 12 (75.00) | 21 (84.00) | 33 | 80.50 |
| III | 32 | 5 | 37 | 25 (71.40) | 3 (60.00) | 28 | 75.70 |
| IV | 20 | 21 | 41 | 17 (85.00) | 16 (76.20) | 33 | 80.50 |
| V | 19 | 21 | 40 | 14 (73.70) | 15 (71.40) | 29 | 72.50 |
| VI | 17 | 24 | 41 | 13 (76.40) | 18 (75.00) | 31 | 75.60 |
| VII | 16 | 9 | 25 | 10 (62.50) | 4 (44.4) | 14 | 56.00 |
| VIII | 24 | 32 | 56 | 20 (83.30) | 23 (71.90) | 43 | 76.80 |
| IX | 22 | 31 | 53 | 15 (68.20) | 20 (64.50) | 35 | 66.00 |
| X | 20 | 8 | 28 | 17 (85.00) | 6 (75.00) | 23 | 82.10 |
| XI | 31 | 31 | 62 | 19 (61.30) | 17 (54.80) | 36 | 58.06 |
| XII | 24 | 32 | 56 | 8 (33.30) | 15 (46.90) | 23 | 41.10 |
| XIII | 24 | 14 | 38 | 18 (75.00) | 11 (78.60) | 29 | 76.30 |
| XIV | 17 | 15 | 32 | 11 (64.70) | 14 (93.30) | 25 | 78.10 |
| XV | 13 | 20 | 33 | 10 (64.70) | 10 (50.00) | 20 | 60.60 |
| Total | 312 | 294 | 606 | 224 (71.80) | 199 (67.70) | 423 | 69.90 |

*Note :* Figures in parentheses are in percentage.

## Training Material

The participants of the training were provided with necessary material like a scribbling pad, a pen, an attractive folder, a handbook on New Panchayati Raj System, and pamphlets on DANIDA scheme. These materials are in vernacular (Tamil) and they are self-explanatory dealing with the DANIDA, its aims, schemes, pre-conditions and the methods by which the schemes can be operated in the rural areas through the Gram Panchayats.

They were also provided with a copy of the 11th Schedule containing the 29 subjects allotted to the Panchayats. The trainees were also given a copy of all the available GOs and they were shown the handbook on the various developmental and welfare schemes of the government implemented by the various departments in Cuddalore district. All essential reading materials have been supplied to them for their use.

**Training Programme Schedule**

The training programme was for a period of two days. On the first day, the participants were oriented in the features of the new Panchayat Raj system, the role of the presidents, vice-presidents, leadership qualities and various developmental and welfare schemes. The details regarding the schemes, categories of beneficiaries, eligibility conditions, names of the departments operating the schemes, the procedures for obtaining the schemes and the officials to be approached to get the schemes have been explained to them. More attention was given on Gram Sabha, decentralisation of powers, people's participation in development process and micro-level planning. The other topics covered during the first day of the training include sustainable development, its meaning and methods.

The second day of the training programme was devoted entirely to the schemes of DANIDA. On the second day, the participants were oriented in the programmes of DANIDA which includes the schemes, approaches, fund allocation, pre-conditions for beneficiaries, type of beneficiaries, subsidies, procedure to get the schemes, component on training the masons, hand-pump and electric pump operators.

**Pre–and Post-Evaluation**

***Pre—Evaluation***

On the first day of the training of each batch, a pre-evaluation test was conducted using a proforma on the new Panchayati Raj system and water and sanitation scheme. These pre-evaluation tests showed that only less than 10 per cent of the participants were aware of a few features of the New Panchayati Raj System. They have indicated the following as features of the new Panchayati Raj System :

1. Rural areas will get more funds from the government,
2. Presidents and vice-presidents have joint responsibility,

3. No need for getting approval from Block Development Officers to implement schemes,
4. Reservation of seats for women,
5. Periodical election,
6. Decentralisation of powers,
7. Direct payment to the last grade staffs by the panchayat presidents, and
8. Gram Sabha.

But the above points were elicited from the participants after repeated probing and help. In general the participants were ignorant of the basic features of the Panchayati Raj System as well as their powers and responsibilities. In the case of women participants their awareness level was very poor. Barring a selected few, all the other women participants had no knowledge about the system and basic facts about their Panchayats. It is really a sorry state of affairs to note that a few women presidents were not able to spell out the names of their Panchayats from where they were elected. Half of the women participants agreed that they have come just to sign the records in the meeting as requested by their husbands and they also revealed that it is only their husbands who look after the entire Panchayat affairs. They could not speak out even the requirements of their Panchayats.

Contrary to the above situation, there were a few women participants who could talk better than the male participants. Some of them listed out the features of the New Panchayati Raj System and demonstrated that they were able to function well. In one case the women village vice-president was more informative than the male president of the same Panchayat. This village vice-president was hopeful of becoming the president of the same panchayat next time.

Similarly, the participants were asked about their awareness about DANIDA and its schemes. Twenty per cent of them said that they had heard about DANIDA. Participants from Chidambaram area were aware of the DANIDA schemes because DANIDA is implementing schemes in those areas. This pre-evaluation was carried out among the participants of all the batches.

### *Post-Evaluation*

At the end of the second day in each programme, a post-evaluation was carried out using a number of methods like debate, discussions, question-answer sessions, making the participants to speak out their opinion about the training, writing their experiences in the training programme on a separate sheet.

The post-evaluation results show that they were able to gather enough information about the role and responsibility of the presidents, features of the New Panchayati Raj System, and Panchayat administration. They expressed their thankfulness to the training team as the training was helpful to know various development and welfare schemes and the methods through which the schemes could be obtained and operated. They strongly opined that hitherto they were not aware of these schemes. They have given assurance that they would make all efforts to get these DANIDA schemes implemented in their villages. In short, they expressed happiness over the training content and the methods followed. They strongly felt that this type of training should have been offered as soon as they assumed charge as presidents as they have wasted the past two and half years without knowing the necessary information akin to the Panchayati Raj administration.

Regarding the DANIDA schemes, the post-evaluation indicated that they were able to understand the meaning and significance of sustainable water and sanitation schemes and the pre-conditions of these schemes. At the end of the second day session, these participants have listed out the requirements of their Panchayats with regard to water and sanitation. They assured the training team that they would collect the people's contribution to get the sanitation scheme from DANIDA.

**Methods adopted in the Training**

A number of methods have been used in the training programme. The methods used were :

(1) Group exercise
(2) Individual assignment
(3) Lecture through OHP
(4) Lecture-cum-discussion
(5) Case illustration
(6) Games
(7) Pictorial representation
(8) Charts
(9) Question-answer method
(10) Role play.

Under group exercise, the participants were divided into three or four groups; each group (with a president or a secretary) was requested to list out points relating to the subjects given to them and some of the topics given to them included leadership qualities, methods of acquiring leadership qualities, developing and sustaining the same qualities, characterisation of a democratic leader and a dictatorial leader and the methods of convening the Gram Sabha. They were also requested to discuss in groups the various problems that will arise in the water and sanitation programme when they are implemented in the villages.

Similarly, the participants were assigned the task of noting down the water and sanitation requirement of their respective village Panchayats. They were also requested to list out individually the problem they have faced in convening the Gram Sabha meeting and also their personal problems (as they felt).

Under pictorial representation the various subjects allotted to the Panchayats were illustrated. The participants enjoyed all these methods and they said that they are useful in the training programme to learn and to retain them in their memory. It is interesting to note that though the participants were elderly persons with rich life experience they have participated in the deliberations with interest in all the simple games during the training programme.

### Feedback and Reflections of the Participants

The participants expressed, as usual, more difficulties in administering development. The presidents were unhappy over the non-cooperative nature of the vice-presidents whereas, the vice-presidents complained against the presidents for their egocentric and authoritarian attitude. In one case, the village president (male) showed antagonism against the vice-president of his Panchayat who happened to be a woman as well as a relative of his. This is mainly because of his ego. Similarly, they complained against the members for their negligence in attending the meetings regularly.

In implementation of schemes, these presidents have expressed their ignorance of many schemes of the government. Even, among the schemes known to them they felt that it is very difficult to get these schemes due to non-cooperation of the officials. But the training had helped them to acquire the knowledge of various schemes and the methods of getting the schemes by adopting proper approach. They also felt that the training helped them to know the various Government Orders relating to Panchayati Raj administration and this has created confidence in them to run the Panchayat effectively. The participants also felt happy that they have gained confidence to meet any official who was hitherto non-cooperative.

Similarly, these participants expressed their dissatisfaction over the perception of the people as people's expectations are increasing in geometrical proportion. They informed that the people are approaching only the presidents of the Gram Panchayats and not the MLAs or MPs to get their grievances redressed.

## Gram Sabha

With regard to convening of Gram Sabha they felt that it is a difficult task. They have adopted so many methods to mobilise people for the Gram Sabha meeting but only about fifty to hundred members, on an average, participated in the meetings. Even in the Gram Sabha meetings, the people demanded the implementation of the decisions taken in the previous meeting. This posited a great problem for them. Similarly, some of the villagers under the influence of alcohol disturbed the proceedings of the meetings. The participants perceived that the training had helped them to approach the people with great faith and confidence. They reported that hereafter they will definitely get more participation in the Gram Sabha meetings.

The latest guidelines of the State government, the proper procedure and rules for organising Gram Sabha have been explained to them. The trainees got a clear-cut picture about the methodology to be adopted to attract the people to the Gram Sabha and they have learnt the art of conducting the proceedings and tackling the queries raised by the members. Importance of Gram Sabha was known to them only through the training for which they profusely thanked the trainers.

The success of DANIDA's demand-driven approach and the people's contribution concept depends on the Gram Sabha and its functions. Hence, sufficient attention was given to this topic in the training programme.

## Resource Persons

Apart from the resource persons from Gandhigram Rural Institute some of the Panchayat presidents who got tremendous success in implementing various schemes including DANIDA schemes, were invited for a discussion. One among them was Mr. Panneer Selvam of Keerappalayam panchayat. These successful presidents shared their experiences with the trainees on the aspects of getting the people's support and share for the successful implementation of the DANIDA schemes in their villages. The participants had a lively interaction with these presidents and this exercise enabled the participants to get more faith and motivation.

Similarly, the mechanics — both hand and motor pump operators — who were trained by DANIDA in the villages, were also invited and they were also asked to share their experiences. Likewise, the user group women from the villages where the DANIDA had already implemented its schemes had also been invited and they were asked to explain and share their experiences with the trainees. All these helped the participants to understand better the DANIDA schemes.

**Other Visitors**

During the course of the training the Block Development Officer (BDO) of Mangalore Panchayat Union and the woman president of the same block Panchayat paid a visit and she had a lengthy discussion with the participants. The panchayat union officials also interacted with the participants and cleared their doubts on administration.

In Virudachalam, the Chief Training Organiser of the Krishi Vigyan Kendra (KVK) also interacted with the participants and explained the various schemes offered by the KVK and he has requested the participants to make use of the KVK programmes for agricultural purposes.

**Women Participants — A Focus**

Women have been trained separately without mixing them with men. Half of the women presidents did not show any interest in the training programme initially. They said that they have nothing to do with the Panchayat administration since it was only their husbands who are looking after the entire activities. Even, for this training they said that they have come just for putting the signature as requested by their husbands. But after a few sessions, women started pouring questions on each and every issue. To the surprise of the training team women came out from their shell and posited critical questions. Their mindset has been changed and they declared that they will act on their own hereafterwards. At the end of the training programme they expressed their happiness over the manner in which the training was conducted and also about the content of the training programme. They felt that this training programme should have been provided much earlier, at least one year before so that by this time they could have emerged as good leaders.

Many women participants had to walk to their villages for a minimum of three to four miles and even then they ventured to sit in the training till the end at the late evening. But the DANIDA took them by its vehicle to their villages as it was late evening. This kind of cooperation extended by the women leaders to the training team greatly helped the DANIDA and the training team. In short, these women presidents were very much satisfied with the training programme.

## Water and Sanitation Programme

During the second day of the training programme in each batch focus was given to DANIDA's Water and Sanitation Scheme. Initially the participants were informed about the DANIDA, its schemes, objectives and approaches. Then, individual schemes were explained to the participants in regard to the pre-conditions, beneficiaries, subsidy component, method of getting the schemes, the concept of user group, the people's contribution and the need for people's contribution, and maintenance of the property.

The participants were requested both individually and in groups to discuss and list out various problems in formulation, implementation, monitoring and maintenance of the schemes. This exercise helped them to understand the problems in general and they were able to suggest possible solutions to such problems.

It is understood from the reflection of the participants that DANIDA has a bright hope to implement its WS schemes in the villages of this district. All the participants have individually requested for DANIDA's help for their villages by giving assurance to the training team that they will ensure people's cooperation in the form of contribution.

During the course of the training programme, a few presidents expressed that they are ready to pay their contribution to get the DANIDA schemes to their villages. With regard to household latrine programme, about 70 per cent of the participants have assured that they would motivate the people for putting up household latrines. Each president has assured a minimum of 25 household latrines to be constructed in their villages initially and on seeing this, others will follow. As for institutional latrines, all the presidents have demanded this programme for their areas. For all the above schemes, the participants have assured that they will convene the Gram Sabha meeting latest by May first week and after the meeting it will be conveyed to DANIDA.

**Significance of Mass Awareness**

The training had helped the participants to understand the need for the New Panchayati Raj System, its administration, and role and responsibilities of the leaders in social development. They felt that they had to face a number of problems in convening the Gram Sabha meetings as the people do not understand the purpose of the meeting. But now, as a result of the training, they have developed confidence and hope to convince the people, and organise the meetings effectively.

Similarly, with regard to the DANIDA schemes, the participants hoped to make the people understand the DANIDA schemes and to get all those schemes to their villages. But at the same time they also informed that people are more receptive to outside officials than to local leaders and hence they requested the team to visit their villages and speak to the people for massive response. This will help them to collect the people's share without much difficulty.

It was also reported by the presidents that it will be difficult for them to go to Cuddalore office frequently for getting the DANIDA schemes. So, they requested to open field offices in their area at least one in Virudachalam, a central place where people use to come more frequently.

**Review Meetings**

The first review meeting of the training programme was conducted on 7th February 1999, in the office of the District Coordinator, Cuddalore. Dr. G. Palanithurai, Training Programme Co-ordinator also attended the meeting. The Chief Adviser and the District Co-ordinator, suggested a few modifications in the training method and requested to involve more games and pictograms. In short, the DANIDA officials expressed satisfaction over the training programme. In the second review meeting which was held on 2nd March 1999, in the District Co-ordinator's Office, Cuddalore, the DANIDA officials expressed satisfaction.

**Follow-up**

The training programme, no doubt, has motivated the participants to take steps to get DANIDA schemes. But it was felt by the training team that immediate follow-up action may be taken up to keep the presidents in touch with the DANIDA schemes and to ensure full participation of the people.

*ANNEXURE 1*

## COURSE CURRICULUM

*First Day*

— Registration / pre-evaluation / ice break
— Introduction to Panchayati Raj — Genesis, importance of Panchayati Raj system
— Salient features of 73rd Amendment
— Tamil Nadu Panchayat Act, 1994
— Powers and Functions of Gram Panchayat
— Powers and Functions of Gram Sabha
— Role and responsibilities of Gram Panchayat Members
— Details of Panchayati Raj administration
— Maintenance of registers and records
— Development programmes for Panchayats and individuals
— Role and responsibilities of the presidents and vice-presidents of Gram Panchayats
— Village planning and participation of the people
— Leadership qualities and traits
— Significance of sustainable development

*Second day*

— Review of the first day programme
— Introduction to DANIDA Water and Sanitation Project concept, objectives, approaches and pre-conditions
— Participatory planning
— DANIDA WS project — implementation process
— Water supply
— Drainage
— Household latrine
— Institutional latrine
— Action plan — drafting
— Sharing sessions with the successful presidents
— Post-evaluation
— Valedictory

*ANNEXURE 2*

## OUTCOME OF GROUP EXERCISE

The participants were given individual as well as group exercise to list out the qualities of a successful leader. This exercise helped them to learn more about the leadership qualities and to identify the weaknesses in their leadership.

The following traits are listed by the participants as qualities of a successful leader :

1. Ensuring the support of the people and officials
2. Understanding the dynamics of groups in the villages and bring out solidarity among various social groups and their leaders for common action
3. Economic independence for their personal life
4. Easily approachable
5. Having adjustability
6. Possessing tender qualities like love, affection, patience, humbleness, non-violence and feeling of togetherness
7. Selfless service
8. More flexibility in approach and action to keep the people together
9. Understanding and accepting one's own defects (self-analysis)
10. Grip over the rules of administration
11. Understanding the concept of development and sustainability
12. Respecting the people's feelings and sentiments
13. Team spirit
14. Open-mindedness and vigilance
15. Tolerance and braveness
16. Keeping oneself above prejudice

## *ANNEXURE 3*

In the group exercises on the qualities of an authoritarian leadership, the following attributes were identified by the participants :

1. Independent decision making
2. Exercising authority
3. Total control
4. Not admitting criticism
5. Threatening others
6. Keeping unquestionable position.

*ANNEXURE 4*

## PERCEPTION OF THE TRAINEES ABOUT THE HARDSHIPS IN ORGANISING GRAM SABHA

1. People are yet to understand the significance of Gram Sabha and only a limited number of members attending Gram Sabha.
2. The opposition group creates problems in Gram Sabha and people believe rumours.
3. The difference of opinion between presidents and vice-presidents persists and it has created a gap among various collectivities.
4. The presidents do not have the organising capacity.
5. People expect more loan facilities.
6. People look at issues in the backdrop of the caste affiliation.
7. People expect fulfilment of the grievances expressed in the previous Gram Sabha meeting.
8. There was no practice among the people to sit and discuss the Panchayat affairs in the distant past.
9. It is very difficult to bring the poor to the Gram Sabha as the poor has to lose their income on the day of the meeting.
10. Alcoholism among the villagers is a menace during the Gram Sabha meeting.

## *ANNEXURE 5*

In the group discussions on finding ways and means for organising Gram Sabha successfully, the following suggestions were offered by the participants:

1. Giving publicity well in advance
   — Door to door canvassing
   — contacting informal groups like women and youth
   — posters/wall writings
   — through public address system information is to be given
   — seeking the help of Ward Members to mobilise the people
2. Keeping the records, audited reports and other necessary documents on the Panchayati Raj administration
3. Encouraging the women members to participate in the Gram Sabha
4. Giving priority to implement the felt needs identified by the people in the previous meeting
5. Responsible in answering the questions raised during the Gram Sabha meetings
6. The president should be equipped with more details of the Panchayat activities as well as the activities of the other tiers and development agencies
7. Display of records in public places, including the previous year income/ expenditure details.

*ANNEXURE 6*

**PARTICIPANTS INTERACTED MORE ON THE FOLLOWING AREAS**

*On the First Day Sessions*

1. The concept and importance of decentralisation
2. Gram Sabha and its problem in its effectiveness
3. The problem of joint responsibilities between president and vice-president
4. Indifferent attitude of officials
5. Lack of enabling facilities to improve the efficiency of Panchayati Raj administration
6. Lack of interest among the members to attend Panchayat Council meeting
7. Poor financial conditions of Panchayats
8. Fund allocation — not need-based
9. Absence of linkages among the three-tier system
10. Political influence — discrimination in fund / scheme allocations
11. Problems in group housing scheme
12. Non-availability of bank loan in spite of subsidy sanction
13. No periodical interaction of the higher officials with the presidents
14. No meaningful discussion or guidance even if meetings are arranged

*Second Day*

1. The role of international funding agencies especially DANIDA in developing Indian villages
2. Approach and pre-conditions of DANIDA people's contribution — problems expected
3. Eligibility conditions for each scheme
4. Demand increased for home connection
5. Lack of voluntarism among people
6. The implementation process of Water and Sanitation about
   - the estimates preparation/contract
   - users group concept
   - keeping of tool kit
   - selection of trainees for HP mechanics and masons
7. Target total estimate (maximum)
8. Enlist minimum number of beneficiaries
9. Technical details on honeycomb model-tanks for household latrines
10. Material : quantity, roofing pattern, cost of material pertaining to household latrines
11. Provision of water supply to school toilets

*ANNEXURE 7*

## PENT-UP FEELINGS SHARED BY THE PARTICIPANTS: INDIVIDUALLY WRITTEN

1. Not able to complete the works as promised.
2. When people make complaint repeatedly on the same problem which could not be solved within the framework of Panchayats.
3. If a large number of demands are brought in the meeting which could not be comprehended.
4. I wish to administer the Panchayat honestly. But I feel restless when people criticise me. I could not act further.
5. In spite of availability of power, I could not execute it.
6. I do not know how to talk to people.
7. My anger is my weakness.
8. People are demanding more and more facilities even though a lot of works have been done for them.
9. People do not attend in large number if public meeting is organised.
10. Financial problem in Panchayats.
11. I do not understand the feelings of the people properly.
12. Shyness.
13. Non-cooperation of members.
14. In the Gram Sabha meeting I have to answer the people's questions however foolish they are.
15. Get angry when things are getting delayed.
16. In general I do not have the ability to adjust with others.
17. Unable to implement the Panchayat schemes effectively.
18. Water supply and sanitation facilities are not provided to the people.
19. People are wasting water. A few sections are not able to collect water.
20. I do not have oratory skill.
21. I feel organising meeting is a hard task.
22. Not able to arrange the loan facilities.
23. Not able to provide group house to the poor.
24. Not able to provide new road.
25. Without informing people through tom-tom, the president organised Gram Sabha. I feel sorry for this.
26. Anger has to be avoided.
27. The explanation to the people must be simple — according to their taste.

28. People do not have understanding power.
29. People believe the propaganda of the opposite groups.
30. People show careless attitude.
31. Feeling shy while meeting people.
32. Have to contact people directly.
33. Have to consult member/vice-president and request them to extend their cooperation.

*ANNEXURE 8*

## WOMEN PARTICIPANTS AND THEIR RESPONSES

1. They felt that the village community does not whole-heartedly accept the women as leaders.
2. Personal constraints — dual responsibility family as well as Panchayat — lack of time.
3. Social inability — lack of knowledge on the local politics, illiteracy.
4. Lack of opportunity to meet others and share their experiences and no common forum to improve their capacity and personality.
5. Male members of the family do not believe the capacity of their women.
6. Alcoholism, gender discrimination are the real hurdles for the women leaders.
7. Find it difficult to contact and convince government officials. In spite of the above difficulties, they felt that women leadership has more advantages like :

   (i) Easily the women are approachable as well as general populace
   (ii) Easily understand women's problems
   (iii) All the time available in the house to meet the people
   (iv) Women feel free to approach the women leaders and pose their demands to be fulfilled
   (v) Easy to spread the message on Health and Sanitation.
   (vi) Less corrupt and less party orientation
   (vii) Honest and patience
   (viii) Women's problems like dowry, harassment can be addressed easily to the women by the women leaders.

*ANNEXURE 9*

## WHAT THEY ARE GOING TO DISCUSS IN GRAM SABHA ON WATER AND SANITATION

1. Discussion will be made in the Gram Sabha about the scope and prospects of DANIDA's scheme to be implemented in the village.
2. Stress on people's contribution — by explaining the importance and advantages.
3. Involving Local Village Associations like Youth, Women and Caste to convince the people.
4. Through the school children message will be given to parents about the need of the scheme.
5. Associating with Village Administrative Officer, cooperatives, teachers and other field staff in the village, the DANIDA programme will be taken to the villages.
6. Sufficient publicity on the WS programmes would be given in the meetings.
7. Contacting and convincing the problematic people in the villages about the scheme.
8. Explain the features like joint effort, Participatory Learning and Action, users group, training components, distribution of tools and equipments to the members of Gram Sabha.
9. Establishing regular contact with women for awareness creation.

## *ANNEXURE 10*

Expected problems in Water and Sanitation programmes in the villages as perceived by the participants in group discussions :

(a) — availability of water source as water level is going down.
— quality of water is always a problem in this area.
— uncleanliness in the surrounding of the water points.
— motor capacity.
— frequent power failure.
— quality of pipes and motor.
— failure of water points due to sand.
— topography of the village — many ups and downs
— storage capacity of the tank — non-availability.
— purification and cleanliness of the tanks.
— distribution of water to all.
— seasonal insufficiency.
— individual disturbance by digging pits.
— water is being wasted while giving connections to individual houses.
— frequent repairs in hand-pumps and motors.
— non-availability of trained mechanic.
— non-availability of equipments, tools and spares.
— poor finance to maintain the institutions.
— more expenses have to be spent for power.

(b) — inadequate drainage facilities
— lack of sense among the people in maintaining the drainage system.

(c) — non-availability of space for open defecation.
— increased awareness among the people on sanitary toilets.

(d) — awareness increased on the need for institutionalised latrines.
— lack of water facilities in the school.

*ANNEXURE 11*

## WATER AND SANITATION DEMANDS BY PARTICIPANTS

An analysis of the water and sanitation requirements revealed that in Nallur Panchayat Union, the presidents demanded the following :

- hand-pumps — both new and repair
- new bore wells
- construction of new OHTs
- repair the existing OHTs
- extension of pipe lines
- support pillars for the water taps
- putting up new pipe lines
- repairing the damaged pipe lines
- electric motor
- household latrines
- drainage facilities and a few institutional latrines.

The major demand in their Nallur Panchayat Union is new hand-pumps and household latrines.

**Mangalore Union**

Majority of the presidents of the Panchayat Union demanded :

- hand-pumps
- OHTs (both new and to repair the old ones)
- motor with motor rooms
- deepening of bore wells
- putting up new pipe lines
- increasing the capacity of the existing tanks
- providing supportive pillars to the water taps
- submersible motor

The major demand of this union was hand-pumps, household latrines, drainage and supportive pillars for the water points

**Virudachalam Union**

- hand-pump

— overhead tank (OHT) — new and repair
— new pipe line
— repairing hand-pump
— new motor
— increasing the capacity of the tank
— household latrine
— institutional latrine.

The major demand is for hand-pump (new) OHT and household latrine.

The demands of other two unions namely Kammapuram and Parangipettai have been indicated in printed cards already submitted to the district office.

## *ANNEXURE 12*

Successful personalities, involved in the implementation of DANIDA Water and Sanitation Scheme, and interacted with the participants were :

| | | | |
|---|---|---|---|
| 1. | Mr. K. P. Pannerselvam | — | President,<br>Keerapalayam |
| 2. | Mr. Ganasekaran | — | President,<br>Ramapuram |
| 3. | Mr. Seethapathy | — | Vice-President,<br>Vattathur |
| 4. | Mr. Umadevan | — | Correspondent,<br>Vallalar School<br>Pattaveli |
| 5. | Correspondent | — | Virudhakeereswarar, ITI<br>Virudhachalam |
| 6. | Mr. Pakkrisamy | — | Mechanic,<br>Keerapalayam |
| 7. | Mr. Kalaiselvam | — | Mechanic,<br>Keerapalayam |
| 8. | Smt. Saraswathy | — | Mechanic,<br>Keerapalayam |
| 9. | Smt. Sudha | — | Mechanic,<br>Keerapalayam |
| 10. | Smt. Santha | — | Mechanic,<br>Nainarkuppam |

*ANNEXURE 13*

## SESSIONS OF INTERACTION WITH SUCCESSFUL LEADERS

The resource persons have engaged the presidents who had already implemented the DANIDA Water and Sanitation programmes successfully in their villages for interaction in the training programme. Their direct interaction with the trainees was fruitful as they were live examples, models and pioneers since they have succeeded in their attempts of achieving cent per cent sanitation.

Many of the problems, difficulties and hardships expected in the implementation of the DANIDA WS have been cleared by the presidents through interactions. The resource persons explained their steps, strategies, approaches in organising the people, motivating them to contribute, establishing relationship with DANIDA officials, implementing the schemes and managing the finance and programmes.

The concept of users group and its functioning was explained in detail. The participants raised questions on the minimum individual contribution to the users group and voluntarism extended for maintenance. Training component for hand-pump and motor-pump mechanism was really appreciated by the participants. The quick and easy process of maintaining water points well attracted the participants. The historic achievement of 100% sanitation in the village of Keerapalayam was a motivating factor to the participants. The possibilities of ensuing support of the village organisation and utilisation of common fund for the DANIDA scheme explained by the resource persons was an eye opener to the trainees.

When the schemes of institutional latrines were discussed, the correspondents of schools shared their experiences and the way in which they managed to mobilise fund from teachers, parents, teachers associations. They have also indicated that by contributing from their own funds they set examples to others.

*ANNEXURE 14*

## TRAINING MATERIAL

1. A hand-book in vernacular on the new Panchayati Raj administration with key features, duties and responsibilities of presidents, vice-presidents and members, village Panchayat duties and responsibilities, affairs like provision of drinking water, sanitation, street lights, television, social justice, economic development of weaker section, women and child care.
2. Notes on the schemes and development programmes pertaining to village development and individual development.
3. A copy of the 11th Schedule containing the 29 subjects allotted to the Panchayati Raj institutions.
4. Three pamphlets on DANIDA and its scheme components, photos, drawing, measurement details and technical guidelines, fund allocation, pre-conditions, subsidy component etc.
5. Sets of Government Orders available were provided to them for copying.
6. A handbook on the Tamil Nadu Panchayat Act, 1994, leaders do's and don'ts, during meeting and proceedings.

# 3

# TRAINING PROGRAMME CONDUCTED FOR GRAM PANCHAYAT PRESIDENTS AND VICE-PRESIDENTS ON WATER SUPPLY AND SANITATION*

## Introduction

The DANIDA administration of the Villupuram district has entrusted the responsibility and task of providing training to the village panchayat presidents and vice-presidents of Villupuram district to the Rajiv Gandhi Chair for Panchayati Raj Studies, Department of Political Science and Development Administration, Gandhigram Rural Institute. Initially, the resource persons of the training team were given an orientation programme on 23rd and 24th January, 1999 by the officials of the DANIDA to make the master trainers have grip over the DANIDA project and its objectives.

The overall objective of the orientation programme was to facilitate the trainers to increase their understanding and knowledge on DANIDA-assisted Demand Driven Water Supply and Sanitation project and to transmit the same to the village Panchayat presidents and vice-presidents in the training programme.

## Objectives of the Training Programme

The objective of the training programme is to enable the presidents and vice-presidents to understand the Panchayati Raj System and its deep implications on the society in the context of 73rd Amendment, their roles and responsibilities. Further, it is intended to equip them to manage the

* Sponsored by DANIDA-II

institution to achieve economic development and administer social justice. This training has to enhance the capacity of the leaders to involve the people in the development process of the society. Basically, this programme has to bring the change of mindset among the leaders to consider development as the outcome of non-government-oriented activities but the result of people-centred activities as in Kerala. But it has a focus mainly on the project of DANIDA namely Water Supply and Sanitation. This training programme will enable the leaders to reap optimum utilisation of the DANIDA scheme and thus, it would contribute to the sustainability of water supply and sanitary facilities created in the rural areas. The specific objectives of the training programme include:

- To create wider awareness about the New Panchayati Raj System — the concept, principles and importance of Panchayati Raj in general and knowledge on Panchayati Raj Act in Tamil Nadu, in particular.
- To familiarise the participants with the task of a village Panchayat and its role and responsibilities within the scope of Panchayati Raj Act.
- To discuss about the various development schemes available for the village Panchayat and individuals and to get maximum utilisation of State and Central resources.
- To develop leadership qualities required to lead, manage and control the community activities and resources and to recognise different leadership qualities required to become successful Panchayat leaders.
- To disseminate information on water and sanitation project — concept, strategy, approaches and criteria for support.
- To expose the leaders to the participatory techniques of planning and executing project activities.
- To develop individual or group action plan to avail assistance from WS project of DANIDA.

**Need for the Training Programme**

The objective of DANIDA WS programme is to provide protected drinking water to all and at all times (on a sustainable basis). The strategy adopted in this programme is Demand Driven Approach. The demand for the water scheme should come from the people. So, the people should be informed about the availability of such a scheme, the pre-conditions and approach to be adopted in this scheme. The assumption is that the village Panchayat presidents and vice-presidents who are always with the people and enjoy the respect and confidence of the people can thereby inform the people about the scheme and get the support of the people for implementing the project in their respective Panchayats. Moreover, they will be able to motivate and help the people to plan and implement the scheme.

Further, DANIDA firmly believes as a policy approach that the village Panchayat as a self-governing institution should take the responsibility of implementing the scheme with the participation of the people. Since the presidents and vice-presidents, as representatives of the people, have a major role in the implementation of the scheme, they should be oriented about the scheme and in turn the representatives can take the messages to the people especially women, discuss with them, motivate and convince them to make use of this opportunity to get the maximum benefits. Against this backdrop it was decided to provide training to the presidents and vice-presidents of Villupuram district as DANIDA operates its WS programme in the above-mentioned district.

**Training Methodology**

Participation of people is considered as key for development. A number of participatory methods were used in the training programme to bring maximum input from the representatives. They are :

- Group exercise
- Individual assignment
- Lecture-cum-discussion
- Case illustration
- Social games
- Role play
- Pictorial representation
- Charts/OHP
- Question-answer method
- Story
- Incidences
- Brief lecture

The training team encouraged the participants to take active participation through unstructured and thought-provoking discussions, and question-answer sessions.

Wherever, the group of participants was small, the trainers used direct individual interaction with them. In case the group was large, the participants were divided into three or four groups. Each group (with a president as a secretary) is made to list out the problems akin to subjects given to them. Some of the topics given to them include methods of acquiring, developing and sustaining leadership qualities, method of convening the Gram Sabha meetings more effectively and successfully, especially to discuss the DANIDA WS scheme and so on. They were also asked to discuss in groups the various problems that may arise in the water and sanitation programme of DANIDA.

Similarly, the participants were assigned the task of noting down the water and sanitation requirements of their respective village Panchayats.

Under pictorial representation, the various subjects allotted to the Panchayats are illustrated. They are also informed about the various Government Orders relating to these subjects. The participants have enjoyed all these methods and felt that these methods are useful in the training programme for easy understanding of the subjects and issues.

**Training Material**

The participants of the training programme were provided with all the necessary materials like, a scribing pad and a pen to note down the key points, an attractive folder, a, hand book on New Panchayati Raj System, pamphlets on DANIDA, its schemes, approaches, a copy of the 11th Schedule containing the 29 subjects allotted to Panchayats, a copy of all the available GOs and a cloth batch. All these materials, in vernacular, were self-explanatory.

**Training Programme Schedule**

Each of the training programmes is being organised for two days. The course content of the first day programme includes the key features of the New Panchayati Raj System, the role of the presidents and vice-presidents, leadership qualities, various development/welfare schemes including the beneficiary categories, eligibility, the names of various departments implementing the schemes, the procedures for obtaining the schemes and the officials to be approached to get the schemes. More attention is being given to Gram Sabha, decentralisation of power, people's participation, micro-level planning and so on.

The concept, meaning and methods of sustainable development are also covered during the first day of the training programme. Gender sensitisation is an important topic discussed in all the training programmes.

But more attention to this issue is given in the batches exclusively meant for women.

The second day of the training programme is devoted entirely for DANIDA's scheme. On the second day, the participants are informed about the DANIDA, its schemes, approaches, fund allocation, pre-conditions for beneficiaries, type of beneficiaries, subsidy, procedure to get the scheme, Participatory Learning Appraisal and component of training the masons, hand-pump and electric motor-pump operators.

**Successful Leaders — Role Models**

The DANIDA has invited some of the Panchayat presidents who have achieved success in implementing various schemes, especially DANIDA schemes, for a discussion with the trainees. These successful presidents shared their experiences in getting people's support and contribution for the successful implementation of DANIDA scheme in their villages. This enabled the participants to have a lively interaction with these presidents and to have more faith in DANIDA.

Similarly, the mechanics—both hand-pump and motor-pump — who were trained by DANIDA in the villages, have also been invited and they also shared their experiences with the participants of the training. The users group women — from the villages where the DANIDA had already implemented its scheme — are also invited and they have explained and shared their experiences with the trainees.

The participants have asked a number of questions such as whether the women mechanics are able to undertake the repair work easily; whether the people would support her in undertaking repair works; where do they get their charges for the repair work done by them; how many days a woman would take to learn this art; and how many hand-pumps have been repaired so far by these women mechanics? The union fitter has tested the knowledge of the women mechanics by asking more technical questions in a training session. The women mechanics have successfully answered all the questions to the surprise of the leaders. After these demonstrations the participants felt happy and satisfied over the training programme. All these helped the participants to understand better the DANIDA and its programmes. They have been motivated to get the DANIDA WS scheme for their villages.

**Other Visitors**

During the course of the training programme, the Union Chairman, the BDO and the EOP at the respective union visited, and participated in the discussion and also interacted with the participants. It is to be noted that the Chairman of Melmalayanur Panchayat Union was present in the training session on both the days. Similarly, the BDO and EOP of Chinnasalem Panchayat Union were present in the session during the entire programme and interacted with the participants.

**Pre-Evaluation**

Pre-evaluation was conducted on the first day of all the training programmes. This was done by using a proforma as well as by question-answer method on the New Panchayati Raj System and water and sanitation scheme. The participants were very poor in their knowledge on the features of New Panchayati Raj System and its implications. Only a few (less than 20 per cent) have stated one or two aspects of the following features :

1. Reservation of seats for women
2. Responsibility of local bodies
3. Gram Sabha
4. Periodical election.

**Post - Evaluation**

At the end of the two days session of all the training programmes a specific time was allotted for post-evaluation. The post-evaluation was carried out with the help of a number of methods like question and answer, debate and making the participants to speak out their learning in the training.

These post-evaluation exercises revealed that the training programme had helped them to gain wider understanding about the features of New Panchayati Raj System — the concept, the objectives, the features, the role and responsibilities of the presidents and vice-presidents, methods of acquiring, developing and sustaining leadership qualities, various welfare/development schemes, the names of departments implementing the schemes, the officials to be contacted to get the schemes and so on. The participants thanked the training team for explaining and guiding them to get a lot of development programmes. Though they were aware of a few schemes, they could not get these schemes, as they did not know the procedures. So, they felt, that this training has helped them a lot to gain more insight into the schemes. They expressed happiness over the content of the training, and the method followed. They strongly advocated that they are too late in receiving this type of training and that this type of training should have been imparted long before, at least one year back. One of the presidents has expressed that the training team was able to make the participants sit continuously for a period of five hours a day which is really a very difficult task in the whole exercise as presidents do not have such practice and orientation.

The post-evaluation exercise indicated that the training helped them to understand clearly the DANIDA, its schemes, pre-conditions beneficiaries, the meaning and significance of sustainable and protected water supply and sanitation. At the end of the second day session, the participants listed out the WS requirements of their villages and they assured that they have gained the confidence of collecting people's share for these water and sanitation schemes of DANIDA.

**Logistics Arrangements**

The logistics arrangements like providing training materials, lunch and refreshments to the participants, accommodation and transport to the resource persons have been carried out with utmost care by DANIDA.

**Training Schedule**

In Villupuram district, a total of 13 training programmes covering six Panchayat Unions have been completed upto 13th May, 1999. The details of dates, venue as well as attendance are as follows :

| Sl. No. | Block | Batch | Total Strength M | F | T | Participants M | F | T | % | Venue and Date |
|---|---|---|---|---|---|---|---|---|---|---|
| 1. | Melmalayanur | 1 | 42 | 12 | 54 | 41 | 6 | 47 | 87 | Melmalayanur 16, 17 April |
| 2. | Mugaiyur | 2 | — | 33 | 33 | — | 15 | 15 | 45 | Thirukovilur 19, 20 April |
| | Mugaiyur | 3 | 46 | — | 46 | 40 | — | 40 | 87 | Thirukovilur 21, 22 April |
| | Mugaiyur | 4 | 47 | — | 47 | 17 | 3 | 20 | 43 | Thirukovilur 23, 24 April |

*Contd.....*

| Sl. No. | Block | Batch | Total Strength M | F | T | Participants M | F | T | % | Venue and Date |
|---|---|---|---|---|---|---|---|---|---|---|
| 3. | Thirukovilur | 5 | 29 | 23 | 52 | 12 | 15 | 27 | 52 | Thirukovilur 3, 4 May |
| | Thirukovilur | 6 | 52 | — | 52 | 35 | 2 | 37 | 71 | Thirukovilur 5, 6 May |
| 4. | Thiyagadurgam | 7 | 21 | 19 | 40 | 17 | 10 | 27 | 68 | Kallakurichi 7, 8 May |
| | Thiyagadurgam | 8 | 40 | — | 40 | 34 | — | 34 | 85 | Kallakurichi 10, 11 May |
| 5. | Thirunavalur | 9 | — | 26 | 26 | — | 16 | 16 | 62 | Ulundurpet 14, 15 May |
| | Thirunavalur | 10 | 62 | — | 62 | 46 | 1 | 47 | 76 | Ulundurpet 17, 18 May |
| 6. | Chinnasalem | 11 | — | 25 | 25 | — | 20 | 20 | 80 | Chinnasalem 19, 20 May |
| | Chinnasalem | 12 | 37 | — | 37 | 27 | 1 | 28 | 76 | Chinnasalem 21, 22 May |
| | Chinnasalem | 13 | 38 | — | 38 | 27 | — | 27 | 71 | Chinnasalem 25, 26 May |
| | Total | | 414 | 138 | 552 | 216 | 89 | 385 | 70 | |

*Source* : Computed.

## Feedback of the Participants

— This type of training should have been given two years back.

— The Union Chairman should be given training with regard to the linkages, support and coordination between village Panchayats and block Panchayats.

— All the participants felt that they could understand the problems relating to water and sanitation and Panchayati Raj administration only after they became presidents.

— Participants felt that it will be more effective if the DANIDA staff meet the people during the time of Gram Sabha meeting.

— The participants evinced keen interest in getting the DANIDA schemes to their villages.

— They felt that all the information provided to them was new to them and was very much useful to them.

— They expressed that the training has given them the necessary courage and confidence. They assured to get DANIDA scheme to their villages.

— Whenever the government convenes the meeting of the

Panchayat presidents, sincerity and punctuality is not adhered to. But this training programme is different from that of the programme conducted by the government.

— The DANIDA can inform about its scheme through TV.
— They have understood the dimensions of the water and sanitation problems.
— The training has helped them to improve their leadership qualities.
— The training helped to them to improve their knowledge on Panchayati Raj administration and to know about various schemes.

**Women Participants**

Three training programmes were conducted exclusively for women participants of three Panchayat unions namely Mugaiyur, Thirunavalur and Chinnasalem. Most of the women participants came either with their husbands or assistants. For any question relating to Panchayat administration they depended on either their husbands or assistants. But all the women participants expressed that they themselves conduct the Panchayat meetings. In all these programmes for women more focus was given on gender sensitisation.

Some of the reflections expressed by these women participants are given below :

They showed keen interest in the training programme. A few of them wanted the training programme for five or six days duration as they have to learn a lot about the Panchayat administration. They expressed that though they have attended a number of training programmes nobody explained in detail like this. They also said that since this is a small group it was very easy to discuss and learn a lot through mutual interaction. In the training programme conducted by the Government officials, there is no discussion but it is full of speeches and words of advice.

They viewed that the Panchayats get better leaders than the MPs or MLAs as they are locally available. Only the women presidents know the needs of the people better than the men presidents and they can try to get and implement the schemes useful to the people. This will help to get more respect for women leaders. One president quoted an example of her own case. Before her tenure, her Panchayat had a male president who did not implement any useful scheme in the Panchayat. As she became the president she was opposed, scolded and belittled in a mass meeting. But after she assumed office, she implemented a number of useful schemes and now the entire community in the Panchayat respects her and supports her.

***Problems faced by the Women Participants***

- People expect that the village problems should be solved immediately. For this, they feel it is difficult to go out without the support of people especially males.
- Because of their being females, others do not listen to them, especially the youths do not listen to the good advice offered by the women presidents and vice-presidents. Mindset of the male has not been changed.
- When these women presidents talk about the people's responsibility in public meetings or in Gram Sabha meetings the people do not accept it. The people feel and believe that the presidents have to bring the doles.
- Due to paucity of time it is difficult to attend to household work. Their work load has been increased.
- The expectations among the womenfolk have enormously increased as women presidents assumed power.
- Generally, as the women do not go out, they lack general awareness about what is going on elsewhere.
- They are not able to have public relationship effectively.
- As women, they feel shy.
- They are not able to function independently.
- They are not able to ride two-wheelers .
- Do not know many schemes.
- Less contact with officials.
- Problems due to alcoholism.
- Communal problems bring lot of difficulties in discharging their responsibilities.

**Group Discussions**

The participants of the training programme of all the batches were divided into groups and they were requested to list out the various problems akin to drinking water and sanitation problems. The problems listed out by them were consolidated and are given below :

- Non-availability of quality water for drinking purposes. Available only hard water.
- Electricity — frequent power fluctuation and power failure.
- Poor quality of pipe line — need for replacement with good quality

of P.V.C. pipe.

— OHT — capacity not adequate — to be increased.
— Cleaning of OHT — not proper and regular.
— Repair of OHT
— Capacity of electric motor — not sufficient.
— Digging pits near the water taps — need for increasing the height of taps
— Chlorinating the drinking water.
— Non-availability of adequate water.
— Water source — not properly and scientifically located.
— Need for timely repair of distribution pipes.
— Insufficient pipe lines.
— Non-availability of OHT and hand-pump.
— Need for new OHT to new human settlements.
— Frequent repair of hand-pumps.
— Topographical problems — ups and downs in the streets
— Upper areas do not get adequate water
— Suggested to follow shift system.
— Non-availability of tools to undertake the repair work of hand-pumps and motor pumps.
— Frequent repair of starters.
— People have to take water from the river.
— In the riverside villages, the bore wells get destroyed during floods.
— Rocky soil — difficult to dig well.
— Insufficient water taps in the streets.
— Wastage of water by the people.
— No unity among the people — causes waste of water.
— Stagnation of waste water due to non-availability of drainage system.
— Need for timely replacement of broken pipes with new quality pipes.
— No sense of responsibility among the workers.
— Distance of water source.
— Poor pathway to water source.
— Damaging water taps and pillars by the people.
— Quarrels on the water tap among the people.
— Failure of bore wells due to officials' careless activities.
— Frequent repair of motors due to carelessness of the workers.

**Sanitation Problems**

— Need for toilets in all the villages.
— Need for drainage in all the villages to prevent diseases.
— Need to prohibit pig rearing in the villages.
— Separate place for dumping the garbage.
— Stagnation of water surrounding the water points.
— Need for creating awareness about the importance of personal and environmental hygiene.
— The village health worker should be instructed to visit regularly.
— Need for household latrine.
— Need for cleaning the drainage regularly.

**Steps suggested to convene the Gram Sabha successfully**

The participants in groups suggested the following steps for convening and conducting the Gram Sabha meetings successfully :

— Information through mike, bit notice
— Street corner propaganda.
— Invite the people by creating awareness in them that it is their solemn duty.
— Inform, discuss with the fans associations, youth club members, women's fora, village VIPs, caste leaders, village elders, more particularly involvement of women.
— Respecting the people by the leaders in the Gram Sabha.
— Exhibit Panchayat budget on the notice board and explain.
— Panchayat financial position has to be made transparent.
— Involvement of ward members formally.
— The president should follow give and take policy, taking into account the village needs.
— Proper approach is needed on the part of the presidents.
— Make announcement in mosques, churches and temples.
— BDO, Union Chairman and Union Councillor should be involved.
— Invite the people by informing that
  (i) the meeting is for the development of the village;
  (ii) to inform about GOs;
  (iii) to inform the people about the various facilities offered by the government;
  (iv) to select the beneficiaries of various schemes;

(v) to identify the needs of the people and to recommend to the officials to fulfil the needs;
(vi) to remove illegal activities;
(vii) to place before the meeting the budget and proposals;
(viii) to identify the village needs;
(ix) to get approval of the people for plan activities;
(x) to inform the people about the new plan activities.

— Arrange cultural activities .
— Meeting should be conducted in a public place (for example, Panchayat Office),
— Direct contact of the president and members with the people.
— Provide refreshments.
— Invite eminent speakers to the meeting.
— Arrange the meetings during festival days.
— Arrange a feast (Samabanthi); it is contributory.
— Organise sports debates etc.
— Arrangement/use of public address system.
— Explain about various schemes with the help of
  — officials
  — audio-visual aids
  — wall posters, notice
  — thandora.
— To inform people about the benefits of schemes through those who had already availed of the schemes.
— Involvement of village workers.
— To fulfil the people's needs that were decided in the previous meeting.
— Arrange/facilitate interaction among the people.
— Simplify the procedures for proper people's approach.
— Explain the procedures in a simple language, understandable to the people.
— Make administration transparent by making the income and expenditure of the Panchayat known to all.
— The president and vice-president should coordinate the people.
— Involve the village volunteers and youth and encourage them for participation in the development activities.
— Invite all the people irrespective of caste or class .
— Create awareness among the people about the importance of Gram Sabha and the need for people's participation.

**Reported Problems in Panchayat Administration**

The participants in their group-discussion reported the following problems in Panchayat administration :

— The Panchayat presidents should participate in the Panchayat union council meeting to express their problems.

— Whether MP fund or MLA fund, it should be allotted on the basis of priority needs decided in the Gram Sabha meeting.

— The presidents should be permitted to pay the amount for the completed work as soon as it has been inspected by the Union Engineer.

— All the works related to financial help to the people, OAP, marriage assistance, community certificate, and birth certificate should be entrusted to the village Panchayats and this will help the people and reduce thc incidence of corruption.

— Just like the funds allotted to the MPs, MLAs the presidents should also be provided with Rs. 5,00,000 (rupees five lakhs) per year.

— To help the poor people, marriage halls be constructed in all panchayats.

— Electricity should be supplied free of cost to the Panchayat.

— As the presidents have to meet the people directly and fulfil the needs, they should be given monthly salary just like the MPs, MLAs.

— All the Panchayat roads should be converted into tar road or cement road depending on the importance of the place.

— The government should meet the expenses of convening the Gram Sabha meeting.

— The interference of Panchayat assistants in the Panchayat administration should be reduced.

— They are not able to meet the needs of the village people due to paucity of funds.

— For all the works like JVVT and housing schemes, the cheques should be given in the name of the Panchayat presidents.

— The vice-presidents demand percentage share in all the works.

— All the resolutions taken in the Gram Sabha meeting should be implemented before the next Gram Sabha meeting; and then only people will attend the Gram Sabha meeting and respect the presidents.

— Every year works are provided again and again only to a few Panchayats and the other Panchayats never get any work. So, the works should be provided to all the Panchayats on the basis of priority needs.

— The procedure of Panchayat administration which was announced during the election in October, 1996, was based on the previous system. But from 1-4-97 the new Panchayati Raj administration has come into effect. This gap of six months caused difficulty in continuing the harmonious relationship between the presidents, vice-presidents and members. If the new system of Panchayati Raj administration has been implemented from October, 1996, this type of difficulty might not be there.

— The responsibility of fitting the hand-pump to be given to the panchayat presidents. In case of repair, the process of informing the union, the union fitter coming to get the hand-pump repaired takes time and it does not help the people.

— To switch on the street lights, the EB does not send any person. In the Panchayats also there is nobody to do the work.

— As the Panchayats face financial problems the government may pay the electricity bill directly to the Electricity Board.

— In general, there is drinking water problem in all the Panchayats and this becomes more acute if we provide house connection. But even then, we are not able to avoid providing house connection because people demand it. This creates uneasy situation.

— When the Panchayat presidents visit the Panchayat union in connection with the works related to IRDP the union engineer, the Chairman and other officials demand some percentage and this forces even the honest presidents to involve in corrupt activities.

— In case of power consumed by street lights and drinking water motor services, the EB does not calculate the correct reading of units; instead it gives the bill with approximate quantity of units and collects a huge amount.

— In a few schemes of the Panchayats, the members do not permit its implementation. These members support the vice-presidents and get the bill sanctioned for works that have not been really executed. This tarnishes the image of the presidents.

— The union Chairman interferes in implementing housing schemes in the villages.

— Adequate funds should be allotted to some works like drainage and tar road.
— Repair works in the buildings of primary schools, noon meal centres, shopping complexes, community centres in the village Panchayat area undertaken with the help of General Funds should be done after the opinion of the respective Panchayat presidents has been obtained. This is because, there are instances of irregularities of money being disbursed even without executing the works.
— The details of poromboke lands, river bed, quarries etc. located within the Panchayat area have not been so far handed over to the concerned village Panchayats.
— Most of the poromboke lands, especially the road to burial grounds, are encroached by some influential persons with the support of revenue officials. Even, if the Panchayats pass resolution to evict the encroachers, it is not possible to do so.
— Every Panchayat should be provided with Rs. 50,000 under 'Nammakku Name Thittam'.
— A meeting of the Panchayat presidents should be convened atleast once in three months and the presidents should meet the District Collector in those meetings.
— The agricultural engineering department should consult the Panchayat presidents while constructing check dams.
— As the presidents have to meet the various departments, their travel expenses have increased. So, their allowances should be increased to Rs. 1000.
— TV maintenance (repair) work should be entrusted at the union level. At present, there are only two TV mechanics for the entire district. But there are 127 TVs in one union.
— Some Panchayats have to pay some arrear amount to the government. For this, the government deducts their arrear amount from the funds allotted to the Panchayats this year. This puts the Panchayats in a difficult financial position.
— 60% amount earned from the PWD tanks has not yet been given to the Panchayats.
— While implementing the schemes/works with MP fund, MLA fund, the presidents and vice-presidents should be consulted.
— The IRDP allotment has been reduced to half during this year and this caused great difficulties.
— The tanks which are under the control of Fisheries Department

should be handed over to the Panchayats and this will enable them to get more income.

— The TWAD works should be implemented in consultation with the concerned Panchayat presidents.

— The Panchayat presidents should be consulted in providing house *pattas* by the Department of Backward Class. Similarly, those who do not possess ration cards or election identity cards in the village should not be given house *pattas* in that village.

— Hand-pumps should be put up depending upon the actual needs of the village, by undertaking a direct survey.

— The EB demands Rs. 5000 to install a new electric post (pole). This should be reduced to one-third.

— The government demands and gets the details of electric poles, street lights and hand-pumps. But, the presidents are not informed about the follow-up activities taken in this regard.

— For every work the presidents have to depend upon the government officials which causes delay.

— Most of the resolutions passed by the Panchayats are returned by the Collector. For some works there is no permission and finance.

— As most of the Panchayats are weaker Panchayats, they are not able to implement any of the resolutions passed in the meeting.

— Due to officials' indifferent attitude, the Panchayats are not able to fulfil the drinking water requirements in time.

— Only eight per cent of the revenue from the plan fund is allotted to the Panchayats.

— There is a GO stating that the Panchayats should purchase electric spare parts only from a particular shop and also only of a particular brand. But these goods are not of good quality.

— During the past 15 years, the union tanks have not been deepened, in spite of repeated requests.

— They are not able to evict the encroachers from the public places.

— Could not get group house after 1996, even after so many attempts.

— Could not get the earmarked fund regularly for the past three years.

— The increase in population has resulted in increased need for drinking water supply. But funds are not increased proportionately to meet the additional water requirements.

— In police cases, the presidents should be treated as neutral.

- — There is more problem due to arrack shops.
- — There is problem in the relationship between the presidents and vice-presidents in matters relating to signatures in cheque, powers and responsibilities.
- — Non-cooperation by the opposition party in implementing schemes.
- — Not able to convene Gram Sabha meetings.

**Leadership Qualities as expressed by the Participants**

- — Patience
- — Honesty
- — Ability to convince others
- — Courage to face the situation
- — Self-confidence
- — Impartiality
- — Habit of self-evaluation
- — Enough knowledge on world affairs
- — Literacy
- — Capacity to execute
- — Democratic attitude
- — Ability to articulate
- — Good contact/relation with people
- — Love and affection
- — Adjustability
- — Sincerity
- — Administrative capability.

**Interaction with Successful Leaders and Individuals**

| Sl. No. | Name | Designation | Name of Panchayat & Union |
|---|---|---|---|
| 1. | Mr. Balu | President | Molasur - Marakkanam |
| 2. | Mr. Agamindran | President | Uppuvelur - Valur |
| 3. | Mr. Kannan | Hand-Pump Mechanic | — do — |
| 4. | Mr. Gunasekaran | President | Vadhanur - Kanadamangalam |
| 5. | Sri K. Ramakrishnan | WS Committee Member | — do — |
| 6. | Mr. P. Parthasarathi | Motor Mechanic | Kanadamangalam |
| 7. | Mr. Sivaraman | President | Sesanganur- Kandamangalam |
| 8. | Mr. Purusothaman | Power & Hand-pump Mechanic | — do — |

*Contd.....*

| Sl. No. | Name | Designation | Name of Panchayat & Union |
|---|---|---|---|
| 9. | Mr. Subramani | Mason | Vadhanur - Kandamangalam |
| 10. | Mrs. Padmavathi | HP users group President | — do — |
| 11. | Mr. Devendran | President | Kedar - Kanai |
| 12. | Mr. Govindan | Mechanic | — do — |
| 13. | Mrs. Uma | Mechanic | — do — |
| 14. | Mrs. Poongavanam | Mechanic | Koliyanur - Koliyanur |
| 15. | Mr. Velavendan | Mechanic | — do — |
| 16. | Sri P. Kuppusamy | President | Vairapuram - Olakkur |
| 17. | Sri D. Elangovan | Hand-pump Mechanic | — do — |
| 18. | Sri K. Mannangatti | Power-pump Mechanic | Kilapakkam - Vanur |
| 19. | Mrs. Sarasu Sekar | President | Naduvananthal - Mylam |

**Experience of Successful Leaders**

*Mr. Balu,* President of Molasur Panchayat, shared his experience as follows :

He said that as a president he attended a meeting organised by the DANIDA where the DANIDA schemes were explained. As his Panchayat required all the facilities, he made up his mind to take the DANIDA water sanitation scheme to his Panchayat. Initially, they needed two handpumps and he met the women groups, youth groups and rich lanlords of his Panchayat and explained the DANIDA schemes to them. To contribute the people's share he collected money as donation from the rich landlords and others. Also he motivated the youth groups and women group members to contribute their mite and to motivate the other people to provide their shares. Thus, he collected Rs. 10,000 and deposited it in the bank. Then DANIDA provided its share and put up two hand-pumps in his Panchayat. Similarly, for the school latrine he collected an amount of Rs. 14,000 from the parents, teachers and other well-wishers and constructed a school latrine at a cost of Rs. 1,40,000 with DANIDAs assistance. He has also motivated the people to construct household latrines and about fifty families had done so. For this he himself prepared the bricks and supplied to the families who have constructed latrines.

*Mr. Agamindran,* President of Uppuvelur Panchayat, shared his interesting experiences with the presidents. In case of drinking water he approached the village headman (Nattanmai) to get his permission to implement the DANIDA scheme. The headman laughed at him and refused. But his repeated attempts and the acute water problem made the people to persuade the headman to permit the president to have DANIDA scheme in their village. Then he started collecting donation and one *muth* (belonging to the Jains) from Karnataka donated Rs.18,000 and also by auctioning the withered trees he was able to contribute Rs. 38,760 and put up 5 hand-pumps provided by DANIDA.

Similarly, in the case of household latrines the people did not believe the subsidy component. So, he put up three model latrines and helped three families to get subsidy. On seeing this, the other families started demanding household latrines and thus, 102 latrines have been constructed. He aims to make the village 100% sanitary village. His approach was to meet the women group first and motivate them. He said that his Panchayat was the first one to implement DANIDA scheme in Villupuram District.

*Mr. Gunasekaran,* President of Vadhanur Panchayat, explained his experience as follows :

He attended a DANIDA meeting and in this meeting he referred to the problem of drinking water in his village. The staff of DANIDA agreed to help in this regard. DANIDA staff visited and explained this scheme to all the people in the village. The President organised a meeting of all VIPs in the village including a group which always opposes all the moves and explained the DANIDA scheme to all the participants. The people questioned about the contribution and they preferred only government scheme. President convinced the people and said that the government programmes are not good and indicated the failures. The people have agreed to contribute for this programme and hence they have started with school latrine programme. Further contribution came from village common fund also and thus, they have completed school latrine at a cost of Rs. 1,00,000.

In the same way the president helped the other hamlets to provide them water facility. He collected donation from the rich people for this programme. The people suggested a place for hand-pump and the DANIDA staff inspected the spot and put up a hand-pump in the place indicated by the people. Earlier, a hand-pump was put up by the Panchayat union at the same place but it did not work since the yield was very poor. These new pumps provided by DANIDA provide adequate and tasty water to all. For drinking water scheme it was very difficult to convince the people first and after repeated meetings with convincing argument it was a success. The people hesitated to take household latrine as they had no knowledge of sanitation.

Frequent meetings with the people and DANIDA staff visits helped the Panchayat to make the people feel about the need for a household latrine. Initially, the president himself purchased all the materials and started constructing toilets in fifteen houses. This model motivated the other families to put up household latrines in their houses. 110 latrines in all have been constructed and no corrupt practice is involved in the process as it is in the government schemes. A few volunteers were selected in each street to collect the contributions of the people. It took one month to convince the people. The number of people attending the meeting slowly increased in subsequent meetings. So far he has completed the works costing Rs. 6,00,000 (DANIDA works).

Now the village has no problem in connection with water and sanitation and he has arranged to collect Rs. 1,600 from each family to put up household latrines with DANIDA subsidy. He has so far provided six hand-pumps and one hundred and ten household latrines and one school toilet in his village areas. Even in his absence, people of his village will cooperate with DANIDA as they came to the conclusion that DANIDA comes to help the people.

*Mr. Sivaraman,* President of Sesanganur Panchayat, narrated his experience as follows :

There were two hand-pumps in his village and both of them failed, so there was acute water problem and the people had to fetch water from a distant place by journeying three or four kilometers with the help of bullock carts and tractors. At this juncture DANIDA scheme was introduced.

He convened the meeting of the members of Gram Sabha with all the important persons, including the womenfolk. He initiated a discussion on water problem with concern as people felt that they can spend money from the village common fund (meant for festivals etc.). Then they contributed their shares and completed the work. They contributed Rs. 45,000 and completed the work at a cost of Rs. 3,00,000. Since it was the felt need of the people, it was done very quickly.

*Mr. P. Kuppusamy,* President of Vairapuram Panchayat, explained that as soon as he returned from DANIDA meeting, he convened the village meeting, discussed in detail about the water problem they faced and the DANIDA scheme. People opposed initially but he convinced them by explaining the severe water problem. He appealed the people to permit him to make use of the village common fund. Though there was opposition he managed to convince them and provided Rs. 20,000 from the common fund. In return they got four handpumps at a cost of Rs. 35,000 each.

*Mrs. Sarasu Sekar,* President of Naduvananthal Panchayat, narrated that the topography of her village was of ups and downs. The upper area did not get water and hence there was acute water scarcity. As the bore well was very deep, the nearby farmers damaged it more frequently and it was very difficult to get the services of the union fitter. So, they were facing this problem for a long time and hence the moment she explained the scheme, the people readily contributed their shares around Rs. 10,000. An amount of Rs. 5,000 was provided from the village common fund and thus a total of Rs. 15,000 were contributed and the DANIDA put up three hand-pumps at the rate of Rs. 35,000 each. Also they have put up 50 household latrines.

*Mr. Devendran,* President of Kedar Panchayat, who was the president of users group on irrigation channel, explained as follows:

His village was taken for research on irrigation pattern by Anna University funded by EEC (European Economic Community) in 1989. They wanted the people to contribute Rs. 50,000 and he collected the amount from the rich landlords. They formed a society and registered it. The benefits of usufructus come to the village and every year, they spent Rs. 30,000 for maintaining the channel.

The society gets a huge income from the trees and 45% of the income is provided to the village and the society retains 55%. This amount is utilised for common purposes. As soon as DANIDA scheme was introduced, the village provided Rs. 30,000 as people contribution and put up six hand-pumps with the help of DANIDA fund. Similarly, the society provided Rs. 20,000 as its share to put up a school latrine.

## BLOCK-WISE REPORTS

The Panchayat union-wise details of the training programme are presented in the following paragraphs.

### I. Melmalayanur Panchayat Union

The training programme for the presidents and vice-presidents of Melmalayanur Panchayat Union was organised on 16th and 17th April, 1999, in the Council Hall of the Panchayat union.

A total number of 54 participants (42 males and 12 females) were requested to attend the training programme. Of the total invitees, 47 participants attended the programme (87%). Among the males 98% of them and among the females 50% of them attended the programme.

The sex-wise literacy level of the participants is given in the following table :

**Literacy level of the leaders**

| Educational Level | Presidents | | | Vice-Presidents | | | Total |
|---|---|---|---|---|---|---|---|
| | M | F | T | M | F | T | |
| Primary | 6 | - | 6 | 10 | - | 10 | 16 |
| Middle | 4 | 1 | 5 | 3 | 1 | 4 | 9 |
| Secondary | 10 | 4 | 14 | 4 | - | 4 | 18 |
| Higher Secondary | 1 | - | 1 | - | - | - | 1 |
| College | 2 | - | 2 | 1 | - | 1 | 3 |
| Total | 23 | 5 | 28 | 18 | 1 | 19 | 47 |

*Source* : Computed.

As this was the first programme for this district (as far as GRI team is concerned) Ms. Nancy, the training expert, DANIDA, Villupuram, introduced the training team to the participants and all the participants introduced themselves. The Union Chairman Mrs. E.Rajarani was also in the programme from the beginning of the training programme.

All the participants were made to speak with no exception. As the venue was not a spacious one, we could not engage them for group discussions; instead we adopted the method of individual interaction with the participants of this group. During the interaction, there were heated exchange of views about the non-cooperation of vice-presidents with the presidents. They were convinced by highlighting the features of their joint responsibility and the need for unity among themselves. The presidents also felt that there is no link between the three tiers of the Panchayati Raj institutions.

An interaction of the participants with the union chairman was arranged and a question was asked as to how can the union chairman establish linkage with the Panchayat presidents? The union chairman answered as follows :

The union chairman was ready and eager to meet all the presidents regularly at least once in a month, discuss about the various schemes and get schemes for their villages. As the presidents cannot get and implement large schemes like bridge, road, etc. they can meet her, discuss and get them priority-wise to their villages. She also assured that she plans the scheme only on the basis of the needs of the Panchayats. So, she said that she can be approached to get schemes for their villages. She wanted the presidents to take her to their Panchayats, show the schemes that are needed and she will do her level best to fulfil the village needs. During this interaction, she revealed that last year, she met the district coordinator,

DANIDA and enquired about the programmes of DANIDA. This means that she is more interested in getting the DANIDA Water and Sanitation scheme to her Panchayat union. She requested all the participants to take the DANIDA schemes to their villages.

**Village Needs listed out by the Presidents and Vice-Presidents**

| Name of the Village | HP | MP | OHT | RHP | RMP | PL | HHL | IL |
|---|---|---|---|---|---|---|---|---|
| Sathananthel | 2 | — | — | — | — | — | 25 | 1 |
| Malthemili | 2 | — | — | 1 | — | — | 20 | 2 |
| Kooduvanpoondi | 2 | — | — | — | — | — | 30 | 1 |
| Paruthipuram | 3 | 1 | — | — | — | — | 25 | 5 |
| Eyyil | 2 | — | 1 | 1 | 1 | Yes | 80 | 2 |
| Karadi Kuppam | 2 | 1 | — | — | 1 | — | 50 | 1 |
| Kodukkan Kuppam | 2 | — | — | — | — | — | 15 | 1 |
| Eeyakunam | 2 | 2 | — | — | — | — | 25 | 1 |
| Kapalampadi | 3 | — | — | 1 | — | — | 25 | 2 |
| Melvayalamur | 3 | — | 1 | — | — | Yes | 25 | 2 |
| Kottapoondi | 2 | 3 | — | — | — | — | — | 1 |
| Nochalur | 3 | — | — | — | — | — | 25 | 1 |
| Sitheri | 2 | — | — | — | — | — | 10 | 1 |
| Siruthalaipoondi | 2 | — | — | — | — | — | 30 | 2 |
| Parayanthangal | 2 | 1 | — | — | — | — | 50 | — |
| Avalurpettai | 5 | — | 1 | — | — | — | 50 | 2 |
| Thalanur | 2 | — | — | — | — | — | 25 | 1 |
| Thurapadi | 2 | — | — | — | 1 | — | 20 | 1 |
| Mananthal | 5 | — | 2 | — | — | — | — | — |
| Malnemmeni | — | — | 1 | — | — | — | — | — |
| Edapattu | 2 | — | 1 | — | — | — | — | — |
| Devanur | 3 | — | — | — | — | — | — | — |

HP—Hand Pump MP—Motor Pump OHT—Over Head Tank
RHP—Repair Hand Pump RMP—Repair Motor pump PL—Pipe Line
HHL—Household Latrine IL—Institutional Latrine

## 2. Mugaiyur Panchayat Union

Three training programmes were conducted for the presidents and vice-presidents of Mugaiyur Panchayat union. All the three programmes were arranged in the Danish Boarding High School at Thirukovilur on 19 and 20, 21 and 22, 23 and 24 April, 1999. Among the three batches, one was exclusively for women participants.

In all 75 participants took part in the training programme of whom 34 were presidents (22 males and 12 females) and 41 vice-presidents (33 males and 8 females). The literacy level of the participants is presented in the following table :

**Literacy level of the leaders**

| Educational Level | Presidents | | | Vice-Presidents | | | Total |
|---|---|---|---|---|---|---|---|
| | M | F | T | M | F | T | |
| Literate | 1 | 2 | 3 | — | 1 | 1 | 4 |
| Primary | 6 | 4 | 10 | 13 | 1 | 14 | 24 |
| Middle | 4 | 4 | 8 | 9 | 4 | 13 | 21 |
| Secondary | 7 | 2 | 9 | 7 | 2 | 9 | 18 |
| Higher Secondary | 1 | — | 1 | 1 | — | 1 | 2 |
| College | 3 | — | 3 | 2 | — | 2 | 5 |
| Technical | — | — | — | 1 | — | 1 | 1 |
| Total | 22 | 12 | 34 | 33 | 8 | 41 | 75 |

*Source* : Computed.

For the women group, importance was given to gender sensitisation and the session was started with this aspect. For the other two batches, the sessions were introduced with self-introduction and by question-answer method.

The women group evinced keen interest in this programme as they wanted the programme for five or six days. They felt it very much useful as they could learn a lot about the Panchayat administration. They appreciated the training as it was a detailed one and as the number was small they could take part in direct interaction with experts. Also as there was no male participant in the group, they were able to talk freely and discuss openly.

The male participants requested that the departments like education, public distribution system and public health should be informed that the Panchayat presidents are empowered to visit and enquire about their activities.

They expressed the view that the presidents should regulate the panchayat activities by joining themselves together and discuss among themselves periodically about Panchayat administration.

One vice-president felt sorry that one day all of a sudden the president took him to the bank and asked him to sign the cheque without any prior information or reason. This created a critical situation for the vice-president.

With regard to the schemes most of them accepted that they were not aware of many schemes. Also they complained about the banks and the DIC that they do not lend money on their request and recommendation for the schemes and programmes even though they were duly approved by the higher authorities.

One more important point put forth by the participants is that the concept of Gram Sabha is very useful. In one village, there was more damage done to agriculture by the pigs. The president discussed about this in the Gram Sabha and with the permission of the Gram Sabha, he shot the pigs in the village. One person lodged a complaint with the police. But the police refused to take action by saying that if anything was decided by the Gram Sabha the police cannot do anything against it.

Generally, the participants showed keen interest in understanding more about the district planning committee and development schemes. In all the programmes there was more discussion on Gram Sabha. They have presented the village needs and they are listed in the following table :

**Village Needs**

| Name of the Village | HP | MP | OHT | RHP | RMP | PL | HHL | IL |
|---|---|---|---|---|---|---|---|---|
| Sennakunnam | — | — | 1 | — | — | — | 15 | — |
| Arumalai | 1 | — | 1 | — | — | — | 96 | — |
| Puthur | 2 | — | 2 | 2 | — | — | 20 | 1 |
| Thandarai | — | — | — | — | — | — | 20 | 1 |
| Alambadi | 2 | — | — | — | — | — | 20 | — |
| Nedungampattu | 5 | — | — | — | — | — | 30 | — |
| Emapperi | 2 | — | — | — | — | Yes | 25 | — |
| Melappoondur | 2 | — | ic | 1 | — | Yes | 25 | — |
| Nerkunmam | — | — | — | — | — | — | 20 | — |
| Surayipattu | — | — | — | 2 | — | — | 25 | — |
| Sadaikatti | — | — | 1 | — | — | Yes | 25 | — |
| Kazhumalam | 6 | 1 | 1 | — | — | Yes | 25 | 1 |
| Othaiyur | 1 | 1 | — | 1 | — | Yes | — | — |
| Thanikolampattu | — | — | repair | 1 | — | Yes | — | — |
| Arcot | 2 | — | 1 | — | — | — | — | — |
| Kadungal | 2 | — | ic | — | — | — | — | — |
| Pilrampattu | — | 1 | ic | 1 | — | — | — | — |
| A. Gudaloor | — | — | 1 | — | — | — | — | 1 |
| Kallanthal | 2 | 1 | repair | — | — | — | — | — |
| Murugampadi | 3 | — | 1 | — | — | Yes | — | — |
| Kadaganur | 2 | — | repair | — | — | — | — | — |
| Devaradiyar Kuppam | 3 | — | — | — | — | — | 25 | — |
| Sithappathogam | 3 | — | 1 | — | — | Yes | — | — |
| Athupandal | 3 | 1 | — | — | — | — | — | — |
| Mugaiyur | — | 1 | 1 | 10 | — | Yes | — | — |
| Sithathur | 3 | — | 1 | 2 | — | Yes | — | — |
| Kandachipuram | — | — | repair | — | — | Yes | — | — |
| Nayanur | 3 | — | — | — | — | Yes | — | — |
| Marankiyur | 2 | — | — | — | — | — | 25 | — |

*Contd. ...*

| Name of the Village | HP | MP | OHT | RHP | RMP | PL | HHL | IL |
|---|---|---|---|---|---|---|---|---|
| Adukkam | — | — | 1 | — | — | Yes | — | 1 |
| Kodungal | 1 | — | — | — | — | Yes | — | 1 |
| Melvalai | 3 | — | — | — | — | — | — | — |
| Adurkalappakkam | 1 | — | — | — | — | — | — | — |
| Veerangipuram | 4 | 1 | 1 | — | — | Yes | — | — |
| Anthili | — | 1 | 1 | — | — | — | 20 | — |
| Kongarayanur | 3 | — | — | — | — | — | 20 | — |
| V. Sithamur | 3 | — | 1 | — | — | — | 75 | — |

HP - Hand Pump
MP - Motor Pump
OHT - Over Head Tank
RHP - Repair Hand Pump
RMP - Repair Motor Pump
PL - Pipe Line
HHL - Household Latrine
IL - Institutional Latrine

ic - increase capacity

**3. Thirukovilur Panchayat Union**

For the presidents and vice-presidents of this Panchayat union two programmes were organised between 3 and 4 and 5 and 6 May, 1999 in the Danish Elementary School, Thirukovilur. In all 64 participants took part in the programme of whom 41 were presidents (29 males and 12 females) and 23 vice-presidents (18 males and 5 females). The details of participants are as follows :

**Literacy Level of the Leaders**

| Educational | Presidents | | | Vice-Presidents | | | Total |
|---|---|---|---|---|---|---|---|
| Level | M | F | T | M | F | T | |
| Literate | 1 | 1 | 2 | — | 1 | 1 | 3 |
| Primary | 9 | 6 | 15 | 7 | 2 | 9 | 24 |
| Middle | 8 | 2 | 10 | 4 | 2 | 6 | 16 |
| Secondary | 7 | 2 | 9 | 3 | — | 3 | 12 |
| Higher Secondary | 2 | — | 2 | 1 | — | 1 | 3 |
| College | 1 | — | 1 | 3 | — | 3 | 4 |
| Technical | 1 | 1 | 2 | — | — | — | 2 |
| Total | 29 | 12 | 41 | 18 | 5 | 23 | 64 |

*Source :* Computed.

The sessions began with a discussion. In both the programmes both male and female presidents participated and the women participants were very much interested in the programme and noted down all the points that were discussed in the programme. Some of the reflections of the participants are :

A few presidents admitted that they do not convene the Gram Sabha meeting due to so many problems like non-cooperation of the vice-presidents and members. Similarly, a few female presidents said that they only put their signatures and all the other activities are carried out by their husbands. In the Gram Sabha, they discussed about the budget, water problem, need for schools, balwadi matters and street lights.

It was also reported by the women participants that in Gram Sabha meetings more women participated and those women who attended the Gram Sabha meeting demanded certain facilities and presidents were asked to fulfil certain needs like school, balwadi, night school and so on. The presidents were satisfied about the women members' participation in the Gram Sabha meetings and thus, it was inferred that there is a good scope for 'users group' and its functioning. One president asked why this DANIDA scheme was not informed earlier? A few presidents, like Kunakkalvadi, were ready to take the DANIDA scheme to their villages at the earliest. In general, the participants evinced keen interest in knowing more about the three-tier system, social justice, reservation of seats for women and leadership qualities in the local body institution.

They felt that the government convenes the meetings of Panchayat presidents. But no sincerity and punctuality is adhered to in such meetings. Some presidents felt sorry that the ward members do not attended the panchayat meetings. They agree the sign the resolutions. Also the participants felt that there is no relationship between the presidents and the BDO/Chairman. The presidents demand that they should be allowed to attend the Union meetings.

Similarly, the Distirct Collector had informed that he will meet all the presidents every Monday after he meets the public. But he never met the presidents and as they went to meet him the Collector asked the presidents to come in queue along with the public.

During the second day there was a good discussion about the people's participation in the drinking water scheme. In the discussion, they have listed out the following needs :

**Village Needs**

| Name of the Village | HP | MP | OHT | RHP | RMP | PL | HHL | IL |
|---|---|---|---|---|---|---|---|---|
| Thimmachur | 1 | — | — | — | — | — | — | — |
| Mudalur | 2 | — | — | — | — | 4 | — | — |
| Villivallam | 2 | — | — | — | — | 5 | — | — |
| Elrampattu | 6 | — | — | — | — | — | — | — |
| Madampoondi | 2 | — | 1 | — | — | — | — | — |
| Aruthankudi | 3 | 1 | — | — | — | Yes | — | — |
| Ariyur | 8 | — | 3 | — | — | — | 20 | 1 |
| Arumpakkam | 2 | — | 1 | — | — | — | — | — |
| Aviyur | 4 | 1 | — | — | — | — | — | — |
| Eravakkam | 2 | — | 1 | — | — | — | — | — |
| Thirupalapandha | 4 | 1 | 4 | — | — | Yes | — | — |
| Thagadi | 4 | 1 | — | — | — | — | — | — |
| Konakkalvadi | 3 | — | 1 | — | — | Yes | 10 | — |
| Koovanur | 11 | — | 1 | — | — | Yes | — | — |
| Poomari | 2 | — | ic | — | — | — | — | — |
| Kattupyur | 3 | 1 | 1 | — | — | Yes | — | — |
| Melthalanur | 4 | 1 | 1 | — | — | Yes | — | — |
| Melmalur | 2 | — | — | — | — | — | — | — |
| Arur | 3 | 1 | — | — | — | Yes | — | — |
| Ja. Sithamur | 2 | 1 | — | — | — | Yes | — | — |
| Meyyur | 1 | — | — | — | — | — | 20 | — |
| Thenakkalanthal | 3 | — | — | — | — | — | — | 1 |
| Nariyanthal | 3 | — | 1 | — | — | — | — | — |
| Ethanmaruthur | 2 | — | 1 | — | — | Yes | — | — |
| Eviyagaram | 3 | 1 | 1 | — | — | Yes | — | — |
| North Nemmili | 4 | — | — | — | — | — | — | — |
| Chola Pandiyapuram | 10 | 1 | — | — | — | — | — | — |
| Sankiyam | 5 | — | 1 | — | — | Yes | 50 | — |
| Venkan | 5 | 3 | — | — | — | Yes | 100 | — |
| Karadi | — | — | 1 | — | — | — | — | — |

HP - Hand Pump
MP - Motor Pump
OHT - Over Head Tank
RHP - Repair Hand Pump
RMP - Repair Motor Pump
PL - Pipe Line
HHL - Household Latrine
IL - Institutional Latrine
ic - increase capacity

**4. Thiyagadurgam Panchayat Union**

Two training programmes (one for males and the other for females) were organised for the presidents and vice-presidents of this Thiyagadurgam Union. The programmes have been conducted on 7 and 8 and 10 and 11 May, 1999, in the Danish Middle School, Kallakurichi. 61 participants (33 presidents and 28 vice-presidents) received this training. The details of the participants are given in the following table :

**Literacy Level of the Leaders**

| Educational Level | Presidents | | | Vice-Presidents | | | Total |
|---|---|---|---|---|---|---|---|
| | M | F | T | M | F | T | |
| Literate | 4 | — | 4 | 4 | 1 | 5 | 9 |
| Primary | 6 | 3 | 9 | 8 | 1 | 9 | 18 |
| Middle | 7 | 3 | 10 | 4 | — | 4 | 14 |
| Secondary | 5 | 2 | 7 | 8 | — | 8 | 15 |
| Higher Secondary | 1 | — | 1 | 1 | — | 1 | 2 |
| College | 2 | — | 2 | — | — | — | 2 |
| Technical | — | — | — | 1 | — | 1 | 1 |
| Total | 25 | 8 | 33 | 26 | 2 | 28 | 61 |

*Source* : Computed.

The Deputy BDO was here in the training programme and interacted with the participants. The copy of the GOs seemed to be new to the participants and they eagerly went through the copy. They said that they have not received the GO earlier. The session was started with a self-introduction by the participants. Some women presidents were ignorant of the new Panchayati Raj institutions. As it was a mixed group of males and females it took long time to explain everything because some female presidents could not understand and respond easily. But they showed more interest in learning more about the Panchayati Raj administration.

The participants suggested that they can minimise the expenditure on festivals and increase the people's contribution for DANIDA schemes. They also expressed the view that (i) involvement of women, (ii) involvement of village organisation/association, and (iii) the involvement of village/caste leader will help in eliciting people's participation in the implementation of DANIDA scheme. They have listed out the needs and they are presented in the following table :

**Village Needs**

| Name of the Village | HP | MP | OHT | RHP | RMP | PL | HHL | IL |
|---|---|---|---|---|---|---|---|---|
| Nagalur | 1 | — | ic | — | — | Yes | — | — |
| Vadapoondi | — | — | — | 1 | — | Yes | 30 | — |
| Pudu Uchimedu | 2 | 1 | 3 | 1 | — | — | 200 | — |
| Thimmalai | 1 | 1 | — | — | — | — | 50 | — |
| Sathanur | 3 | — | 1 | — | — | — | 25 | — |
| Kakshakudi | 1 | — | 1 | — | — | Yes | 20 | — |
| Sithathur | — | — | 1 | — | — | — | 15 | — |

*Contd. ...*

| Name of the Village | HP | MP | OHT | RHP | RMP | PL | HHL | IL |
|---|---|---|---|---|---|---|---|---|
| Koonthalur | 3 | — | 1 | — | — | — | 20 | — |
| Ogaiyur | 3 | — | — | — | — | — | 75 | — |
| Vanjaram | 1 | — | 1 | — | — | — | 20 | — |
| Eranji | 1 | — | 1 | — | — | — | 40 | — |
| Mudiyanur | 2 | — | 1 | — | — | — | — | — |
| Sirunagalur | 2 | — | 1 | — | — | — | — | — |
| Chinna Mampattu | 4 | — | 1 | — | — | — | — | — |
| Pallagacheri | 2 | — | 1 | — | — | — | 75 | — |
| Mudiyanallur | — | — | — | — | — | Yes | — | — |
| Ninnaianur | 1 | — | 1 | — | — | — | — | — |
| Asakalathur | 2 | — | 1 | — | — | — | 50 | — |
| Kokkarayapalayam | 4 | — | 1 | — | — | — | 300 | — |
| Gurupeedapuram | 2 | 1 | 1 | — | — | — | 25 | — |
| Koothakudi | 4 | — | 2 | — | — | — | 25 | — |
| Vadathorasalur | 8 | — | 2 | — | — | — | — | — |
| Peelamedu | 2 | 1 | 1 | — | — | — | — | — |
| Panayakkal | 2 | — | 1 | — | — | — | 25 | — |
| Madam | 2 | — | 1 | — | — | — | 25 | — |
| Nayanur | 2 | — | 2 | — | — | Yes | — | — |

HP - Hand Pump
OHT - Over Head Tank
RMP - Repair Motor Pump
HHL - Household Latrine
ic - increase capacity
MP - Motor Pump
RHP - Repair Hand Pump
PL - Pipe Line
IL - Institutional Latrine

## 5. Thirunavalur Panchayat Union

Of the two training programmes, one was exclusively for women participants. In all 63 participants participated (34 presidents and 29 vice-presidents). The details of the participants are given in the following table:

### Literacy Level of the Leaders

| Educational Level | Presidents | | | Vice-Presidents | | | Total |
|---|---|---|---|---|---|---|---|
| | M | F | T | M | F | T | |
| Literate | — | — | — | 3 | — | 3 | 3 |
| Primary | 3 | 5 | 8 | 13 | 2 | 15 | 23 |
| Middle | 6 | 5 | 11 | 1 | 3 | 4 | 15 |
| Secondary | 8 | 2 | 10 | 4 | — | 4 | 14 |
| Higher Secondary | 3 | — | 3 | 1 | — | 1 | 4 |
| College | 2 | — | 2 | 2 | — | 2 | 4 |
| Total | 22 | 12 | 34 | 24 | 5 | 29 | 63 |

*Source* : Computed.

The programme for women started with an introduction to the need for training with more emphasis on gender sensitisation. The BDO of the block Panchayat was present in the training programme. Most of the women participants (presidents) came either with their husbands or assistants. But at the end of the training programme all the women participants expressed that the training has given them enough courage and faith to face any situation, particularly to run the Panchayati Raj administration more effectively.

During the course of the training, there was a lively discussion and they questioned the need for the third tier of the new Panchayati Raj institution. They also expressed that the people do not attend the Gram Sabha meeting but they are ready to sign at request.

They felt happy that all the information provided to them was new and useful. Some participants felt that the subsidy of Rs. 2000 for the household latrine is low. Also they suggested that the training given to the motor mechanic by DANIDA has to include all aspects like repair of jet pump, coil rewinding etc.

The following Panchayats were interested and ready to pay their contribution to take DANIDA scheme immediately :

1. Vellore
2. Sendanadu
3. Kalamaruthur
4. Kalavanur
5. Nachiyarpettai
6. Sumananthal
7. T. Orathur

They have listed out the needs of their areas and they are given in the following table :

**Village Needs**

| Name of the Village | HP | MP | OHT | RHP | RMP | PL | HHL | IL |
|---|---|---|---|---|---|---|---|---|
| K. Kallakuruchi | 2 | — | — | — | — | — | — | — |
| Sirunapattu | — | 1 | — | — | — | — | 25 | — |
| Deviyanathal | 2 | — | 1 | — | — | Yes | 20 | — |
| Nachiyarpettai | 1 | 1 | — | — | — | — | 20 | — |
| Eranthai | — | 1 | — | — | — | Yes | 20 | — |
| Sumananthal | 1 | 1 | — | 1 | — | — | — | — |

*Contd. ...*

| Name of the Village | HP | MP | OHT | RHP | RMP | PL | HHL | IL |
|---|---|---|---|---|---|---|---|---|
| Pandur | 2 | — | — | — | — | — | — | — |
| Nagar | 1 | — | 1 | — | — | — | 100 | — |
| Mettathur | 2 | — | 1 | — | — | Yes | 20 | — |
| Odaiyananthal | 3 | — | 1 | — | — | Yes | 40 | — |
| East Maruthur | 6 | — | 1 | — | — | Yes | — | — |
| Thirunavalur | 4 | 1 | — | — | — | — | 25 | — |
| Kalavanur | 2 | — | 1 | — | — | — | 5 | — |
| Mathiyanur | 5 | 1 | 1 | — | — | Yes | 15 | — |
| Easwara Kandanalur | 4 | — | 1 | — | — | Yes | 25 | — |
| Vanampattu | 1 | 1 | 1 | — | — | — | — | — |
| Kalamaruthur | 6 | — | 1 | — | — | — | 15 | — |
| T. Orathur | — | 1 | 1 | — | — | Yes | 15 | — |
| Velur | 7 | — | 3 | — | — | — | 10 | — |
| Senthanadu | — | — | 1 | — | — | — | 20 | — |
| Sathanoor | 2 | — | — | — | — | — | 20 | — |
| Semananthur | 4 | — | 1 | 1 | — | — | 20 | — |
| Kampattu | 1 | — | — | — | — | — | 25 | — |
| Nannavaram | 1 | — | 1 | — | — | Yes | 20 | — |
| Audikudi | 2 | — | 2 | — | — | — | 30 | — |
| Urambakuppam | — | — | 1 | 1 | — | — | 25 | — |
| Athoor | 3 | 1 | 3 | — | — | — | 25 | — |
| Aathanur | 1 | — | 1 | — | — | — | — | — |
| Poo. Mampakkam | 4 | 2 | 1 | — | — | Yes | 15 | — |
| Nachiyarpettai | 2 | 1 | — | — | — | Yes | 25 | — |
| Parikkal | 4 | — | — | — | — | — | 30 | — |
| Ba. Killanur | 1 | 1 | — | — | — | Yes | 20 | — |
| Semaenthal | 4 | — | 1 | — | — | — | 20 | — |
| Meppuliyur | 3 | — | 1 | — | — | — | 15 | — |

HP - Hand Pump
MP - Motor Pump
OHT - Over Head Tank
RHP - Repair Hand Pump
RMP - Repair Motor Pump
PL - Pipe Line
HHL - Household Latrine
IL - Institutional Latrine

## 6. Chinnasalem Panchayat Union

Three training programmes (one for females and two for males) were conducted for the presidents and vice-presidents of Chinnasalem panchayat union. These programmes were conducted in the danish Elementary School, Chinnasalem during 19, 20 and 21, 22 and 25, 26 May, 1999. The details of the participants are given in the following table :

**Literacy Level of the Leaders**

| Educational Level | Presidents | | | Vice-Presidents | | | Total |
|---|---|---|---|---|---|---|---|
| | M | F | T | M | F | T | |
| Literate | 1 | 2 | 3 | 3 | 1 | 4 | 7 |
| Primary | 8 | 2 | 10 | 11 | 1 | 12 | 22 |
| Middle | 8 | 3 | 11 | 6 | 5 | 11 | 22 |
| Secondary | 7 | 4 | 11 | 6 | 1 | 7 | 18 |
| Higher Secondary | — | 1 | 1 | — | — | — | 1 |
| College | 2 | — | 2 | — | — | — | 2 |
| Technical | 2 | — | 2 | 1 | 1 | 2 | 4 |
| Total | 28 | 12 | 40 | 27 | 9 | 36 | 76 |

*Source :* Computed.

In all the three programmes, the BDO and the EOP were present, interacting with the participants. The women participants felt that they have taken the political responsibility whereas, the men do not take the family responsibility. The participants of this union seemed to be more interesting, more experienced and influential persons with high status in their villages. They also revealed that it is very difficult to answer the questions raised by the people in the Gram Sabha.

They also reported that grants are released based on 1991 population. But as the population has increased they are not able to manage with that fund. These presidents want the details of all poromboke lands of their Panchayats. So far this information has not been provided to them. They expressed the view that the DANIDA staff should visit their villages, speak to the people about the scheme and this will have a good impact. Most of the participants felt that this type of training should have been given two years back.

All the participants showed interest in getting the DANIDA scheme for their villages. They have listed out the details of needs and they are given in the following table :

**Village Needs**

| Name of the Village | HP | MP | OHT | RHP | RMP | PL | HHL | IL |
|---|---|---|---|---|---|---|---|---|
| Kookaiyur | 25 | — | 5 | — | — | — | 100 | — |
| Rayapanur | 5 | — | 1 | — | — | Yes | 50 | — |
| Ulagakathan | 5 | — | 1 | — | — | Yes | 200 | — |
| Thagamtheerthapuram | 2 | — | 1 | — | — | Yes | 50 | — |
| Pethanur | 3 | — | 1 | — | — | — | — | — |

*Contd. ...*

| Name of the Village | HP | MP | OHT | RHP | RMP | PL | HHL | IL |
|---|---|---|---|---|---|---|---|---|
| Senpakuruchi | 2 | — | 1 | — | — | Yes | 50 | — |
| Thengiyanatham | 3 | — | 1 | — | — | — | — | — |
| Karunkuli | 2 | — | 1 | — | — | Yes | 50 | — |
| Ulagiyanallur | 3 | — | 1 | — | — | — | 100 | — |
| Rayarpalayam | 1 | — | 1 | 4 | — | — | 25 | — |
| V. Mamanthur | 1 | — | 1 | — | — | — | 25 | — |
| Eeriyur | 1 | — | — | — | — | Yes | 20 | — |
| Kalasamuthiram | 2 | — | — | — | — | — | 25 | — |
| Ammaiyagaram | 2 | 1 | 1 | — | — | Yes | 55 | — |
| Painthathurai | 2 | 1 | 1 | — | — | — | 25 | — |
| Mattigaikuruchi | 4 | 1 | 1 | — | — | Yes | 25 | — |
| Moongilpadi | 2 | — | — | — | — | — | — | — |
| Thensettiyenthal | 2 | — | — | — | — | — | 25 | — |
| Bakkampadi | 3 | — | 1 | — | — | — | 100 | — |
| Kallanatham | 5 | 1 | — | — | — | Yes | 50 | — |
| Mattinakuruchi | 4 | — | — | — | — | — | — | — |
| Thottapadi | 1 | — | 1 | — | — | — | 25 | — |
| Pandiyankuppam | 3 | — | — | — | — | — | — | — |
| A. Vasudevanur | 4 | — | — | — | — | — | 100 | — |
| Namasivayapuram | — | — | — | — | — | — | 50 | — |
| Thensiruvallur | 4 | — | 1 | — | — | — | — | — |
| Karunthalakuruchi | 4 | — | — | — | — | Yes | 15 | — |
| Melanariyappanur | 2 | — | 1 | — | — | — | — | — |
| Thimmapuram | — | — | — | — | — | — | 25 | — |
| Nallathur | 4 | — | 2 | — | — | — | 25 | — |
| Pethasamuthiram | 5 | — | — | — | — | Yes | 25 | — |
| Nainar Palayam | 7 | -- | — | — | — | — | 300 | — |
| Karanur | — | 1 | 1 | — | — | — | 40 | — |
| V. Alampalam | 3 | 1 | 1 | — | — | — | 30 | — |
| Anumananthal | 2 | 1 | — | — | — | Yes | 30 | — |
| Elavadi | 2 | 1 | — | — | — | Yes | 50 | — |
| Eesanthai | 2 | — | — | — | — | — | — | — |
| Kural | 2 | — | — | — | — | Yes | 50 | — |
| Thagarai | 5 | 1 | — | — | — | Yes | 50 | — |
| Kadathur | 2 | — | — | — | — | — | 20 | — |
| Vetiperumalagaram | 5 | 1 | — | — | — | Yes | 100 | — |
| Earvaipattinam | 2 | 2 | 1 | — | — | — | 200 | — |

HP — Hand Pump
OHT — Over Head Tank
RMP — Repair Motor Pump
HHL — Household Latrine
MP — Motor Pump
RHP — Repair Hand Pump
PL — Pipe Line
IL — Institutional Latrine

# 4

# TRAINING PROGRAMME CONDUCTED FOR WOMEN PRESIDENTS OF GRAM PANCHAYATS IN FIVE DISTRICTS OF TAMIL NADU*

Women presidents, who have been elected to Gram Panchayats as presidents, are virtually novices in the art of governance and especially managing the institution in which they are leaders. Everywhere, it was reported that 33.3 per cent of the reservation of seats for women has been appropriately utilised by our politicians (men) in substituting their wives or sisters or relatives as they are deprived of contesting the election. The women, majority of them at the last tier, contested the election not on their own but at the behest of someone from their families. Rarely, women are unopposed. After the election, the elected women leaders who have rich social and economic background managed to assert their position everywhere but poor, uneducated, socially and economically backward women leaders are facing hell of problems in managing the institution and in administering development. It is a general belief among the men after seeing the dismal performance of the women leaders that women will be a liability rather than an asset in the local bodies. They know nothing and they are in the hands of their husbands and other male family members. Officials have denigrated the women leaders and they were disrespected. The reason for the disregard of the women leaders is the poor capacity of the women in managing the institution. Hence, it was felt that it is necessary to capacitate the women leaders and their mindset has to be changed and with this aim it was decided to organise two-day training programme with the help of the Central Social Welfare Board. It was organised by the Tamil

* Sponsored by Social Welfare Board.

Nadu Social Welfare Department with the faculty support of Rajiv Gandhi Chair for Panchayati Raj Studies, Gandhigram Rural Institute. Initially, it was decided to organise such a programme in five districts, namely, Thiruvarur, Virudhunagar, Theni, Dharmapuri and Namakkal.

In the training programme, the details about the dimensions of the New Panchayati Raj System, role of women in the New Panchayati Raj System, the need for reservation of seats in the local bodies for women, the role and responsibilities of the leaders in the institution, economic activities in the rural areas, administering social justice, and micro-level planning have been explained. Special emphasis on the present status of women in the society and especially in the local bodies, relationship between the women leaders and the officials, relationship between the leaders and councillors, problems faced by the women leaders in the Panchayat Council, in the offices, in the family and in the society have been highlighted. How to tackle all those problems has been extensively discussed in the training programme with the help of the experienced resource persons and activists.

The whole of the training programme was conducted in a dialogue mode. A number of questions have been raised by the participants and all their questions have been answered satisfactorily. After completing the entire programme covering five districts, it was felt that the impact of the training programme has to be found out. In the training programme, reading material consists of the salient features of the New Panchayati Raj System and the Government orders passed by the Tamil Nadu Government with regard to devolution of powers have been provided to the leaders for their reference.

To find out the impact one-day review workshop was organised in all the five districts. They have been asked to reply to the question as to what extent the training offered by the Social Welfare Department was helpful in discharging their role and responsibilities in the local body institutions. Their answers are as follows :

1. Before taking this training we had entertained fear in our mind as and when we met the officials. We refused to sit in front of the officials even before the clerk. To put our signature on any document of the government office, we had to consult our male family members. Whenever we faced the crowd, we became jittery. When we received letters from the office, we first sought the support of somebody to read the letters.
2. We never had the training of speaking at the public meetings.

How to develop conversation with others was not known to us. How to sit in the midst of the leaders on the *dais* was not known to us. We never had the feeling that we are leaders and we have to lead the society.

3. To go to various government offices and to discuss with officials, we felt that we need someone to guide and support. When the officials talked about rules, regulations and maintenance of accounts we felt that we have assumed these onerous responsibilities without having basic qualifications. While seeing the problems faced by the men in the offices we felt that we don't have that requisite capacity to manage the institutions.
4. When we went to offices, the officials used to discuss all Panchayati matters with our male family members unmindful of our presence. Really, we felt that we lack basic qualities of a leader. Most of the occasions, we did not follow the official instructions as our husbands had been listening to the directions of the officials carefully.
5. We refused to face the crowd and we used to avoid meeting people in crowd. We had been debating in our minds as to whether we had taken right decision or not. So we were in confusion, suspicion and fear.

But after taking this training programme, many changes have been witnessed in our personality and approach. The changes are as follows :

1. We have no fear and shyness.
2. We use to sit in the chair in front of the crowd.
3. We use to speak in the meetings by using the public address system.
4. We move freely with officials without any fear.
5. Without the help of the family members, we visit offices and meet officials.
6. We have not relied on our husbands as it creates troubles.
7. We have learnt the art of organising and mobilising the people.
8. We are in a position to confront the officials if they are not helping and cooperating with us.
9. We have organised self-help group.
10. We are sensitive towards women issues.
11. We prefer to function independently.
12. We have learnt "how to work with the people?"

13. We have now achieved motivation.
14. We have learnt lessons to perfect our personality.
15. We know what is going on in the government?
16. We know our role and responsibilities in the local bodies.
17. We have a feeling of a leader with a sense of commitment towards the society.

These are the changes they have indicated in their personality due to the training they have undergone. It is the beginning of a change in the rural areas with the intervention of the women leaders.

**Training Team**

| | | |
|---|---|---|
| *Coordinated by* | : | The Social Welfare Board<br>*Chairman* : Mrs. Geetha Viswanathan<br>and Officials of the Board and<br>Officials of the Social Welfare Department |

*From Rajiv Gandhi Chair for Panchayati Raj Studies*

| | | |
|---|---|---|
| *Trainers* | : | Dr. G. Palanithurai<br>Mr. M. A. Thirunavukkarasu<br>Officials of Local Bodies of the Districts |
| *Total No. of Leaders Trained* | : | 825 |

# 5

# TRAINING PROGRAMME CONDUCTED FOR PANCHAYAT LEADERS OF TWO DISTRICTS ON POPULATION, HEALTH AND SOCIAL DEVELOPMENT*

## I. Background

In recent times, much emphasis is being placed on decentralisation of authority to the grassroot level elected bodies for local self-governance since these have been accepted as the micro-level instruments of change and social development. In 1993, the Government of India appointed an expert group to draft a national population policy. It suggested a paradigm shift and conceptualised population policies within the context of overall social and economic development with greater devolution of authority and responsibilities to the Panchayats. Towards the end of 1993, the 73rd Amendment Bill was passed giving the Panchayati Raj institutions a constitutional sanction. This was expected to provide the Panchayats opportunities for better management of local resources for their balanced and rational utilisation to plan and implement the need-based programmes and manage or generate additional resources according to their needs and priorities.

In the eleventh schedule of the amendment, 29 items have been listed by way of responsibilities of the Panchayats. Many of these overlap and only three of them directly, and only two partially related to health, family planning, MCH care, etc. Surprisingly, the registration of vital events such as births and deaths, infant and under five-year child mortality, etc., does not find a mention in the assigned responsibilities.

---

* Sponsored by Population Foundation of India.

The devolution of authority has placed a great responsibility on the Panchayats as planning, prioritising or implementing the social development programmes call for certain level of expertise and skills, which the new members may not possess. On the other hand, the task of training and reorienting the large number of Panchayat members may require innovative approaches to be able to reach all of them. The enormity of the task can be judged from the fact that there will be around 3.5 million Panchayat members to be trained with about a million of them being women.

## II. Basic Issues

1. The members of the Panchayats need to be educated, motivated and trained about their rights and responsibilities. Considering the wide divergences and the element of heterogeneity in their social, economic and educational backgrounds it may turn out to be a difficult task. Moreover, around one-third of these would be women members who, traditionally being housewives and mothers, will assume new role of decision-makers for welfare and development activities. This will imperatively call for innovative training strategies and approaches.
2. Reportedly, all the States have set up training institutes for the Panchayat members. Presumably, their number, capacity to handle a large group, training content and methodologies and professional competence would be inadequate to undertake such a task. Training institutions under the Government generally get bureaucratised whereas the need would be to be innovative and flexible. Moreover, the number of Panchayat members in every State would be far greater than any network of training institutions in any State can conveniently handle.

Considering above factors, a need was felt to evolve suitable strategies and methodologies for training of the Panchayat members including development of training material and the self-teaching training aids. It may be pertinent to mention at this stage that the primary focus of the training programmes has to be on empowerment of the Panchayati Raj institutions to enable them to perform their role effectively rather than on training of the individuals. Besides, the methods of training need to ensure long-term sustainability of the programme which can be achieved with an effective follow-up and evaluation system.

There is an urgent need to inform, train and motivate the members of Panchayats on the issues related to female literacy, public health, including water supply and sanitation, nutrition, family planning and women's status, resource management for rational utilisation, preservation of natural resources and generating resources.

In order to discuss and develop various aspects and methodology of training to be adopted, a workshop was convened at M. S. Swaminathan Research Foundation on Training and Project Design for Empowerment of Panchayati Raj Institutions in issues of Population, Health and Social Development on 27-29 January, 1997 at Chennai.

Based on the methodology developed at the workshop, the Population Foundation of India decided to commission a project on training of Panchayat leaders in seven districts, namely, Dharmapuri and Dindigul (Tamil Nadu), Chitradurga (Karnataka), Pune (Maharashtra), Lalitpur (Uttar Pradesh), Sawai Madhopur (Rajasthan) and Bankura (West Bengal). The need for such a project was felt because the number of Panchayat members was so large in the country (around 3 million) that no State training system under the Government could handle it within a reasonable time. Therefore, innovative approaches to cover all the Panchayat members had to be evolved, using training resources and potential outside the Government.

## III. Objectives of the Project

- To train the Panchayat members on issues related to reproductive health, family planning, population and environment, nutrition, maternal-child health care, control of communicable diseases and resource planning.
- To demonstrate the efficacy of the methodology of training of Panchayat members in one district through training a number of local level trainers by an implementing agency (a non-governmental organisation) with the support and guidance of a major consulting organisation for each State.
- To develop video programmes, training manuals and guides, modules, systems for supervision and management information systems, etc., for their wider application.

## IV. Methodology

The methodology of the project developed by the Population Foundation of India and tried in different districts, comprises the following :

1. Identification of a Consulting Organisation (CO) in a State.

2. Identification of an Implementing Agency (IA), a non-governmental organisation in the selected district as the Implementing Agency. In Tamil Nadu, Gandhigram Rural Institute is a consulting organisation and CHERU and Satyamurthy Foundation are implementing organisations for Dindigul and Dharmapuri districts respectively.
3. Training of Implementing Agency members by a Consulting Organisation in the State in various aspects of population, reproductive health including family planning, gender issues, nutrition, environment, control of communicable diseases and structure of the health services.
4. Development of suitable literature in the form of modules on each of the above listed subjects. Also production of a 3-3½ hours video programme based on real life situations on the subjects dealt with in modules, to be used in training.
5. Identification and training of Resource Persons at the community level who could be entrusted with the task of training of Panchayat members in their own villages by distributing literature, showing the video programme and initiating discussions on what the Panchayats could do (each Resource Person would cover 3-5 Gram Panchayats).
6. The local Resource Persons would visit each village once a week, and train the village Panchayat members collectively, covering one area at a time.
7. A mid-term evaluation would be done to identify problems and constraints, to incorporate necessary modifications.
8. Final evaluation and pooling of significant experience for formulating packages of programmes for wider application.

The above methodology has certain inherent advantages, as described below:

— It would ensure training of all the Panchayat members in their own village situation which, in a way, means empowerment of the Panchayati Raj institution.

— A cadre of trained Resource Persons would be available for continuous interactions for three or four months.

— It would help to upgrade the capabilities of the Implementing Agency in undertaking similar training programmes on other responsibilities of the Panchayati Raj institutions.

— It would help to leave behind a corps of trained resource persons who can always be depended upon by the Panchayats even when the project is withdrawn from the area.

— All the Panchayat members in a district can be trained in three or four months, using printed literature in the local language and modern communication technology.

## V. Responsibilities of Consulting Organisations, Implementing Agencies and Resource Persons

### 1. *Consulting Organisations (CO)*

— The Consulting Organisation would be responsible for identifying a lead NGO in the selected district.

— It would organise a workshop of three to five days duration for all Zilla Parishad nembers and the lead NGO, on the various topics connected with the project. The purpose of the workshop would be not only to inform and train the Zilla Parishad members on the various aspects of population, family planning etc., but also to train the NGO personnel and to develop educational material to be used by the NGO and the Resource Persons.

— The CO would also conduct a workshop of three days duration at the district headquarters in the selected district along with the NGO and selected Resource Persons. This may be done in one or two workshops depending on the number of persons to be trained.

— The CO would monitor one training programme at the village level conducted by the NGO and the Resource Persons.

— The CO would conduct a mid-term workshop of three days duration with the NGO and the Resource Persons to evaluate the effectiveness of the various educational materials used, effectiveness of the methodology of training etc. A few selected Panchayat members, who had been trained, should also participate in the workshop.

— The CO would be responsible for carrying out an evaluation through survey of a sample of Panchayat Members trained under this project at the village, block and district levels and assess the impact of the project, and prepare a final report on the project.

— The CO would be responsible for identifying the indicators to be used for monitoring and evaluation of the project at periodical intervals and would be responsible for compiling necessary data from the lead NGO.

– They will also prepare and submit to the PFI a quarterly report on the progress of the project, taking account of the report submitted by the lead NGO.

2. ***Function of the Lead Implementing Agency (IA) in a District***

— The lead Implementing Agency would be responsible for identifying the Resource Persons in the district in different villages and blocks, who can be used for training of the Panchayat members at the village level.
— The lead Implementing Agency should participate in the workshop and training programmes organised by the CO and assist in the preparation of educational materials needed for the training of Panchayat members.
— The lead Implementing Agency would be responsible for conducting training programmes for all the Panchayat Samiti members along with the concerned Resource Persons.
— The lead Implementing Agency would also supervise and assist, wherever possible, in the training rogrammes of the Resource Persons at the village level. They can also organise — workshops for Resource Persons according to the needs, but not more than once in a quarter.
— The lead Implementing Agency should liaise, in the educational and training activities, with the concerned officials of the Zilla Parishad and the Panchayat Samiti. They should supply to the CO regular information on various training activities carried out by them during the quarter including information on number of training programmes held, number of persons trained, etc.

3. ***Resource Persons***

— The Resource Persons would participate in the workshops and training programmes organised by the lead NGO. Their incidental expenses will be covered from the project fund.
— Each Resource Person would be responsible for a group of villages. He would visit the villages assigned to him/her at regular periodical intervals and conduct training programmes with the educational materials made available to him/her.
— He would report to the lead NGO on the activities carried out by him/her in order to get necessary honorarium.

**Dindigul and Dharmapuri Projects**

As mentioned earlier, the districts of Dindigul and Dharmapuri were chosen to implement the project.

The total number of Panchayat members elected in the two districts is mentioned below :

| District | ZP Members | | | Panchayat Samiti Members | | | Panchayat Members | | | Total |
|---|---|---|---|---|---|---|---|---|---|---|
| | T | M | W | T | M | W | T | M | W | |
| Dindigul | 23 | 15 | 8 | 232 | 151 | 81 | 2697 | 1797 | 900 | 2952 |
| Dharmapuri | 41 | 27 | 14 | 420 | 274 | 146 | 5121 | 3414 | 1707 | 5576 |

T —Total; M — Men; W — Women.

The project took off in April 1997. The Gandhigram Rural Institute was identified as the Consulting Organisation for both the districts, while the Council for Health Education and Rural Upliftment (CHERU) and the Satyamurthy Centre for Democratic Studies were chosen as the Implementing Agencies (IA) in Dindigul and Dharmapuri respectively.

Following identification of the various agencies to be involved in training, a series of meetings and discussions were held, where the methodology to be tried out was discussed in detail and a detailed plan of action drawn up. The following activities were carried out from July 1997 onwards.

***Orientation Meetings***

The Consulting Organisations (CO) organised training programmes in July 1997 for the master trainers from the two Implementing Agencies. Side by side, orientation programmes were also conducted for the Zilla Parishad and Panchayat Samiti members, to sensitize them to the issues being tackled in the project, and to get their active support in the Panchayat members training programmes, later on.

***Development of Training Material***

Seven modules were developed in Tamil by the CO, for distribution amongst all levels of Panchayats and the Resource Persons (RPs). The topics that were covered were :

- — Clean water and good health
- — Antenatal and natal care
- — Postnatal care
- — Communicable diseases — their spread and prevention
- — Women's Rights
- — Modern Contraceptives
- — Population and Environment.

A video documentary was also prepared on all the 7 modules. The video film depicted the existing conditions in rural areas and explained the ongoing Government programmes on the related topics. The master trainers were given sufficient orientation to equip them to undertake the task of training the Resource Persons, using the above mentioned training material.

***Selection and Training of Resource Persons (RPs)***

Resource Persons were identified and recruited from the respective blocks for the training programme. The criteria adopted for selecting the Resource Persons included their willingness, educational background, capability in organising and undertaking training, familiarity with the local conditions, previous experience in training/social work, etc. After selection of the Resource Persons, 3-day training programmes were organised by the Consulting Organisations (CO) and the respective Implementing Agencies (Dindigul / Dharmapuri). The programme was residential in Dindigul. The training programmes were intended to provide orientation to the participants not only on the selected topics, but also in organisational and methodological aspects of the training programmes. District and block level officials also attended some of the training programmes. The training schedule provided information on the Panchayati Raj System, created awareness in the selected topics, discussed rural situation and details of Government programmes and welfare measures. Pre- and post-test evaluation was conducted to gauge the capabilities and awareness of the volunteers and the effect of the training. It was found that after the training programme, the Resource Persons were sufficiently equipped to carry out the prescribed task.

***Panchayat Members' Training Programme***

The Implementing Agency at the district level (CHERU and Satyamurthy Centre for Democratic Studies) approached the district and block level officials and appraised them about the training programme. They sought the cooperation and support of the Government officials for the successful implementation of the programme. The officials, in turn, instructed their subordinates at different levels to extend their support and cooperation.

The selected Resource Persons were given the responsibility of organising and conducting training programmes in their respective areas. Each Resource Person was made responsible for training 5-6 Gram Panchayats. As a first step, the Resource Persons approached the Gram Panchayat officials and the Gram Panchayat president and briefed them about the training programme. In consultation with them, convenient dates and venues for training at the Gram Panchayat level were decided. The Resource Persons were responsible for making the necessary arrangements, conveying the training dates to the Panchayat members, distributing the modules, and showing the video cassettes. In most of the areas, training was organised at the Gram Panchayat level. Apart from the Resource Persons allotted to each Gram Panchayat, the Implementing Agency staff also supervised the training programme from time to time. The CO was also involved in monitoring the training programme.

The Resource Persons usually covered 1-2 modules each day, in each Gram Panchayat. It took around 2-3 months to cover all the modules with 6-8 visits in each GP. During the course of training, it was felt that a second round of training would be beneficial, as for most of the Panchayat members, this was their first exposure to health issues. A mid-term evaluation was conducted in February 1998 to gauge the effect of the training, which was followed by a second round of training of the Panchayat members.

Screening of the video cassette was comparatively easy in Tamil Nadu, compared to other States. Since TVs were available in most of the GPs, and supply of electricity was not erratic, only a Video Cassette Player (VCP) was needed to be hired. In some villages, the cassette was shown on the Cable TV network too. Usually, video-screening was done in the evening, so that most of the villagers could gather and benefit from the show.

The Resource Persons underwent a re-orientation training before the second round of training for Panchayat members. The second round of training of Panchayat members was completed in August-September 1998.

### *Evaluation of the Training Programmes*

After completion of the second round of training, the effectiveness of the training methodology and impact of training was evaluated. The main objectives of the end-of-project evaluation were :

— To assess the efficacy of the strategy adopted for the project.
— To assess the effectiveness of the training modules and video cassette in creating awareness and motivation and developing skills.
— To assess the performance of the Resource Persons.
— To assess the Panchayat members' views about the project and its effectiveness.
— To identify the strengths and weaknesses of the project and lessons learnt.
— To plan for extension of the project to the districts.

A detailed evaluation report is available with the PFI and Consulting Organisation. Some of the salient findings are presented below :

**1. Training Methodology**

The strategy of identifying and training local Resource Persons, who would in turn train Panchayat members, was found to be satisfactory. Both the Resource Persons and PMs were satisfied with the venue, frequency and duration of training. The Panchayat members received information about the training programme from either the Panchayat Presidents or the Resource Persons themselves. On certain occasions, the district collectorate, too, took initiative to inform the Panchayat members, by issuing a circular. The training programmes were organised in the Panchayat offices or block headquarters, both of which were convenient for the Panchayat members and Resource Persons. The dropouts from the first round got another chance to attend the training when the second round was organised.

Close monitoring of the programmes by the respective Implementing Agencies was slightly difficult, as budgetary provisions had not been made for extra staff or travel. In Dindigul, however, this was overcome by CHERU by giving the Resource Persons self-addressed post-cards on which the latter sent weekly reports. The CHERU staff then randomly selected some of the post-cards and made surprise visits to the villages. At times, however, the CO staff were also present during the training sessions or video showings.

**2. Training Material**

The training modules had been read by all the Resource Persons and most of the Panchayat members. They found the topics useful, informative and relevant. Some of the changes/additions to be incorporated were suggested by the Resource Persons and Panchayat members themselves:

— could be made more informative
— illustrations may be added, especially for the neo-literate
— in addition to Tamil, the modules may be prepared in Kannada/ Telugu for those with different mother tongues.

The video cassettes were found to be an effective medium of communication. A lot of suggestions, however, were received on how to improve the video cassette, some of which are mentioned here :

— The long lectures need to be shortened and more discussions may be incorporated.
— Songs and local drama may be used to make it livelier.
— Both positive and negative impacts of common practices may be incorporated.

### 3. Performance of Resource Persons

The performance of the Resource Persons was found to be satisfactory. As most of them had a previous experience in conducting training programmes, they did not face much difficulty.

*Number of Resource Persons*

| Resource Persons | Dindigul | Dharmapuri |
|---|---|---|
| Men | 39 | 13 |
| Women | 11 | 87 |
| Total | 50 | 100 |

The Resource Persons were found to be very committed workers, as in certain difficult hilly areas, they had to travel long distances by foot to reach the villages, often carrying the training material and VCP. 40-50 Panchayat members were trained by each Resource Person.

The level of knowledge and skill of the Resource Persons was found to have significantly increased after conducting the training programmes. In some villages, they have initiated changes, together with the Panchayats, for development of the villages.

## 4. Training of Panchayat Members

115 Panchayat members in Dindigul and 135 in Dharmapuri were interviewed for the final evaluation. Nearly 89 per cent of the Panchayat members attended the training programmes. All literate members have read the training modules and found them to be useful and interesting. Some of the Panchayat members have already started using the knowledge gained through the training, *viz* :

— they are propagating the legal age at marriage for both boys and girls.
— they are monitoring the noon meal centres and attendance of both teachers and students in schools.
— cleaning water tanks and chlorinating them regularly.
— checking the functioning of the ANM.
— some Panchayats have motivated the villagers to arrange for a vehicle for transfer of emergency cases to hospitals.
— putting up garbage cans in the village and mobilising the youth to dump the garbage in pits, away from the village.

The Panchayat members have expressed the view that the training programme would help them to address health and related issues while planning developmental programmes for their villages.

## 5. Strength and Weakness of the Project and Lessons Learnt

The experiences of PFI, in implementing the project in the different States, have been varied. Depending upon the socio-economic and cultural backgrounds, geographical landscape, political awareness, and also the commitments of organisations and the individuals involved (CO, Implementing Agency and Resource Persons), experiences have been very different. For example, in the southern States, where literacy rates are higher and political awareness is greater, and the involved organisations fully committed, it has been easier motivating the Panchayat members to attend the programmes. On the other hand, the *purdah* system in the north, together with lower literacy and awareness levels, made it very difficult to identify women Resource Persons, and getting the women Panchayat members to attend the training programmes. Showing of video cassettes has also been difficult, due to lack of electricity, in most of the States. Hiring of a TV, VCP and generator is too costly and the project had made no provisions for the same, presuming electricity would be available.

Monitoring of the project by both the CO and Implementing Agency was found to be difficult in all the project areas, as very often the villages were away from metalled roads and quite distant from where the Consulting Organisations (CO) Implementing Agency was based. The number of staff and transport facilities were also found to be inadequate to cover the length and breadth of the districts.

However, in spite of the practical difficulties encountered while implementing the project, it was generally observed that the methodology was well accepted, both by the Resource Persons (RPs) and Panchayat Members, (PMs). The PMs found it easier to attend the programmes as they did not have to lose their daily earning to travel long distances to training centres. Also, the small doses in which they were imparted the knowledge (1-2 modules/day/week) was found to be acceptable. Both the Resource Persons and PMs found the informal atmosphere to be more congenial in imparting knowledge, where questions could be asked and problems tackled. Certain measures, if incorporated, however, would definitely improve the effectiveness of the training methodology. These are :

— The State Government has to be more fully involved in the programme. They should get the Health Department geared up so that the PHC gets actively involved in the project.

— The Block Development Officers can get the Gram Sevikas to extend support to the GPs and Resource Persons during the training programmes.

— Instead of each Resource Person single-handedly training 5-6 Gram Panchayats (i.e. 50-60 Panchayat members), a team of Resource Persons (2-3) may be formed to provide the training at the cluster level, clubbing 2-3 GPs together as was done in Chitradurga district in Karnataka and Lalitpur in Uttar Pradesh.

— Panchayat members should be trained immediately after they are elected into office and refresher training should be organised every 6 months. This will facilitate their using the required knowledge and skills for the maximum possible time.

— Other than health issues, other topics like agriculture, social forestry, education, non-conventional energy, micro-planning, Government schemes including poverty alleviation programmes, small saving schemes and general administration may also be included.

## 6. Future Plans

The State Governments may take up this methodology, after making the necessary adaptations, while planning their Panchayat training programmes. Given the available infrastructure and other resources with the Government, this methodology may be more effective and less time consuming (as training takes place simultaneously in the various villages/ clusters).

# 6

# TRAINING PROGRAMME CONDUCTED FOR THE ELECTED WOMEN REPRESENTATIVES OF URBAN LOCAL BODIES*

## Introduction

Reservation of seats in the local body institutions for the women in all positions as per the provisions of 73rd Amendment to the Constitution of India, no doubt, is going to create a metamorphosis in the activities of women in polity, economy and society, in the years to come. The initial apprehensions and doubts over the readiness of womenfolk to come into power-centres and to take up responsibilities of administering development on their own, have been dispelled by their participation in the electoral process of the local body institutions in the month of October, 1996.

The elected leaders of the local bodies in Tamil Nadu have started functioning in their respective domain. While discharging their duties they found problems due to various reasons. Of them lack of training is more visible when compared with other problems they face. The rule of the game should be taught to them in order to make the elected leaders handle the office carefully and effectively so as to deliver goods properly to the people. Against this background an administrative training was conceived and carried out throughout the State. But it does not stop with teaching rules and regulations relating to the functioning of the local body institutions. The effective functioning of the leaders fully relies on the leadership qualities of elected representatives. The elected women representatives who have stepped into the portals of power need leadership training essentially. Hence, a programme was conceived to offer leadership

* Sponsored by Tamil Nadu Institute of Urban Studies.

training to the elected women of urban local bodies.

**Designing of the Course**

To design the training course, to prepare the course material and to train the resource persons, three meetings were held in Tamil Nadu Institute of Urban Studies, Coimbatore by involving the three agencies : Gandhigram Rural Institute (GRI), Avinashilingam Institute for Home Science and Satyamurthy Centre for Democratic Studies which were selected for offering training to the leaders. The three institutions have shared the responsibilities in contributing to the preparation of the training manual. The GRI has helped the Tamil Nadu Institute of Urban Studies to evolve a common course. Instructions have been given to all the three training institutions about the content to be offered during the training programme. After evolving a common programme the three institutions have embarked on the training programme in their respective areas.

Assistant Directors of Town Panchayats and Regional Directors of Municipal Administration in the respective areas have taken the responsibility of making logistic arrangement for training in the areas which come under their jurisdiction. Faculty members and resource persons used to take classes for the elected women representatives. Though it is a day programme, the content of the programme is a well set package. From 10.00 a.m. to 5.00 p.m. with a lunch break of one hour is not enough to carry out the package. Yet it has been carried out with great difficulty.

**Training Content**

The training programme has the following course content: a detailed discussion on the background of 74th Constitutional Amendment Act, the salient features of 74th Amendment Act, and the role of women in administering development in their areas, in utilising the powers conferred on them through the 12th schedule.

Emphasis was given more on the responsibilities of the leaders than on powers. Further, a detailed explanation was offered to distinguish executive and legislative functions of the institutions. The conventional belief of the people that the local bodies are to provide facilities has been changed by emphasising the new responsibility of achieving growth, development, social justice and equity apart from providing the facilities. Further, it was explained that the role of the government has been changed. The Government is going to be a facilitator not a provider. The community has more responsibilities and thereby State is reducing its powers and size. Thus, local body institutions assume greater responsibilities. A few of the modern management techniques have been explained to them. More specifically, explanations have been offered to the elected leaders as to how they could work for economic growth and development rather than in building infrastructure facilities alone. The stress was on the small government approach and people's responsibilities. It was also stressed in the training how people could be trained in citizenry in the ward meetings. Further, illustrations were given to inculcate democratic spirit and culture in the minds of the people at the grassroot level. While indicating all the powers mentioned in the Act, one would feel that more responsibilities have been given to local bodies beyond their capacity. Further, it was emphasised that capacity of the women leaders should be enhanced to meet the challenges which they face every day in the local areas.

Visuals have been projected through overhead projector about the challenges the women leaders have to face at present while discharging their duties. Solutions have also been offered to all those challenges. Likewise, the available urban development schemes have been explained to them with all details, by quoting the sources for their references. Adequate care was taken to operationalise the powers given to the urban local bodies through the 12th Schedule. The trainees have been asked to note questions while listening to the lectures and they have been requested to pass their questions in the discussion session which started usually by 3.30 p.m. It went upto 5.00 p.m.

After giving all the above information the representatives have expressed their observations.

**Participants' Observations about the Training**

1. No doubt it is a confidence-building exercise.
2. After listening to the lectures, we as women look at issues more deeply and critically. Our common-sense approach is dead and gone.
3. After this leadership training we are conscious of our leadership rather than gender. This programme gave us orientation to look at issues as leaders not as women.
4. The mind set of the women leaders that women are to represent the women issues has been changed. Now we feel that we are only representatives of the people.
5. We came to know the women issues more deeply only after this programme.
6. We have realised the importance of the reservation of seats for

women in local bodies only after listening to the lecture on "Why reservation for women in local bodies?"

7. So far we talked much about the powers to be devolved but after this programme we felt the onerous responsibilities of the elected leaders in administering development.
8. After attending this programme we feel that our capacity today will not be enough to meet the challenges and it should be enhanced.
9. This programme has cleared our doubt as to whether the elected leaders can assume executive functions.
10. Now we started realising the need of harmony between the elected leaders and functionaries for successful functioning of local bodies to meet the aspirations of the people.
11. After listening to the lectures in the programme we came to know the bundle of programmes for the development of the poor. So far we were in the dark.
12. After this programme we have realised the gap between the perception of the government and the people on efforts at development.
13. This programme educated us about the importance of resource mobilisation on our own to manage our local affairs without depending much on the fund from the State and central government for the sustainability of the local body institutions.
14. This programme has opened our eyes to look at the opportunities provided by the government to mobilise the resources locally.
15. We have realised the importance of communication skill for our success.
16. The present fund position should be improved to meet the aspirations of the people.
17. We came to know that for social development of the local areas more than funds, leaders skill and work are essential.
18. This programme has educated the leaders as to how the leaders have to educate the people about their role and responsibilities in the community.
19. This programme has educated us as to how to inculcate the democratic spirit in the minds of the people through conducting meetings of the bodies.

**Elected Leaders demand more details on the following**

1. All the schemes for urban development should be in the form of

a book.

2. We should know how to conduct women entrepreneurship programme.
3. We need more input on micro-level planning.
4. We need more flexibility in administrative procedures.
5. We feel that more schemes have to be evolved area specifically rather than receiving them from the above.
6. We need orientation of the officials as they are in a different mindset that the officials know everything and people's representatives should be educated and trained by the officials.
7. We need some honorarium for our work. Otherwise, people will involve in corruption or only the affluent section can alone come forward to serve the people through local body institutions.
8. We need more information on the self-employment and entrepreneurship opportunities for women.
9. We need information to build women's organisations and cooperatives.
10. We need training once in six months.
11. They need more models.
12. They need more field visits.
13. They need regular information dissemination through a newsletter or magazine.

**The Pressing Problems in their hands**

1. Corruption in the offices.
2. Irregularities in public distribution system.
3. Drinking water facility.
4. Garbage clearance.
5. Sanitation.
6. Negative attitude of the officials towards the elected leaders.
7. Repairing of roads.
8. Encroachment of the commons by private individuals.
9. Paucity of funds.

**Training Setting**

Programme should not be for the sake of programme and reporting. It has more specific objectives. The officials, not all, there are exceptions, by and large have been trained to conduct programme for reporting. Of course, halls, public address system, food and refreshment have been provided just like for a wedding ceremony. For any training exercise, atmosphere is more important. The hall, public address system, the training material should create a feeling in the participants that they have come for a serious purpose. First, training atmosphere could be created in the training place. It needs no money. It requires seriousness on the part of the organiser. The organiser's presence is also essential. The faculty felt that in some places organisers have taken keen interest in organising the programme. Organiser and his team were very much with the trainees. In most of the places organisers were not in the premises of the training centre and some subordinates attended the work without knowing the importance and implications of the programme. This needs a serious review.

## Conclusion

The representatives of the people to the local bodies have now realised that they have more responsibilities than was the case before attending this programme. The concept of power and authority had distorted the vision in the beginning. While explaining their responsibilities to create responsible citizens, they realised their tasks and works. It is an exercise to change the mindset of the womenfolk who have reached the portals of power. But, this is only a beginning. This exercise has to continue. In the initial stage, for all training programmes, institutions with faculty have been involved. But, in the years to come, the elected leaders who undergo training at present should be the master trainers. They are the pioneers in breaking new path for development. They are the agents of social transformation. This has to go a long way to achieve the objective of empowering the women for gender equity.

### *Coverage*

| | |
|---|---:|
| Districts covered | 16 |
| Leaders trained | 2150 |
| Total No. of Municipalities | 47 |
| Total No. of Town Panchayats | 267 |
| | |
| Representatives from Municipalities | 525 |
| Representatives from Town Panchayats | 1625 |
| Total | 2150 |

# 7

# INTERFACE AND INTERACT PROGRAMME ORGANISED IN KERALA FOR GRAM PANCHAYAT PRESIDENTS OF TAMIL NADU*

**I. Gram Panchayat Visited**

(a) Erattupetta Panchayat
(b) Poonjar Thekkekara Panchayat
(c) Melakavu Panchayat

**II. Block Panchayat Visited**

(a) Erattupetta Block Panchayat

**III. Leaders contacted and interacted**

| | | | |
|---|---|---|---|
| (a) | Block Panchayat President | : | Mr. Noufal Thambi Rawuther |
| (b) | Erattupetta Gram Panchayat President | : | Mr. P. K. Aleyar |
| (c) | Melakavu Panchayat, Vice-President | : | Mr. George Mathew |
| (d) | Poonjar Thekkekara, Panchayat President | : | Mrs. Minerva Mohan |

**IV. Schemes Visited**

— Road laying

* Sponsored by Population Foundation of India

- — Checkdam Construction
- — Drinking water well construction
- — Housing scheme
- — Constructing a market place

**V. Gram Sabha attended**

(a) Erattupetta Panchayat Ward - I
(b) Poonjar Thekkekara Panchayat

**VI. Staff from Rajiv Gandhi Chair**

*Faculty*
Dr. G. Palanithurai
Mr. V. Ragupathy

*Research Associate*
Mr. K. Tamilarasan

*Assistance*
Mr. P. Rajendran

**VII. Reporter**

Mr. G. Prabakar, Editor, Panchayat News

**VIII. Staff from Centre for Rural Management**

*Faculty*
Dr. Jose Chathukulam
Mr. R. M. Abdul Rahim

*Assistance*
Mr. Antony Raj (Interpreter)

**IX. Gram Panchayat President from Tamil Nadu**

P. Manimegalai — D. Gudalur Gram Panchayat
S. Susheela Janakiraman — Koolampatti Gram Panchayat
A. Muthusamy — T. Pudupatti Gram Panchayat

| | | |
|---|---|---|
| S. Ramaraj | — | Tandikudi Gram Panchayat |
| V. Irudhayam | — | Karisalpatti Gram Panchayat |
| A. Perumal | — | Vadugampadi Gram Panchayat |
| T. Rajammal | — | Munnilakkottai Gram Panchayat |
| A. Aalis | — | N. Panjampatti Gram Panchayat |
| K. Vijaya | — | Kappiliyapatti Gram Panchayat |
| P. Periyasamy | — | Veriyappur Gram Panchayat |

**X. Animators from Tamil Nadu**

| | | |
|---|---|---|
| M. Sureshkumar | — | D. Gudalur Gram Panchayat |
| V. Karupaiah | — | T. Pudupatti Gram Panchayat |
| G. Rajendran. | — | Tandikudi Gram Panchayat |
| A. Velankanni | — | Karisalpatti Gram Panchayat |
| K. Palusamy | — | Vadugampadi Gram Panchayat |
| S. Ravikumar | — | Munnilakkottai Gram Panchayat |
| A. Bhaskaran | — | N. Panjampatti Gram Panchayat |
| D. Sivakumar | — | Nehru Youva Kendra |

The first day began with a prayer in the Conference Hall of C.C.M. Tourist Home, Erattupetta at 8.30 a.m. and followed by a briefing about the programme by Dr. G. Palanithurai. He has focussed the mission of the visit and underlined the responsibilities of the presidents and the animators in the whole programme and reiterated the works that are to be performed in their respective Panchayats after their visits in Kerala. After the briefing, Dr. Jose Chathukulam, Director of the Institute of Rural Management, Kottayam, highlighted the Kerala model of development by explaining the people's plan for development. In his lecture he underscored the implications of people's participation and more particularly he explained the social development achieved in Kerala. Kerala Panchayats' structure, function and performance have been unequivocally presented and in the same way people's campaign for planning was highlighted. This introductory lecture enabled the Gram Panchayat presidents and the animators to have a clear-cut picture about Kerala development process. In his lecture he indicated the role of the people in every sphere of development activities. He demystified the concept of planning in his lecture. Thus, the presidents and animators have been given a picture about the role of Panchayati Raj institutions in the development process of the State.

From the conference hall the team proceeded to Erattupetta Block Panchayat office where the team met the president and council members of the Block Panchayat along with the officials. The Block Panchayat president explained the new system and the linkages among the three tiers of the local government. It was fortunate that he spoke in Tamil as he is a Tamil Musalman migrated from Tamil Nadu long back. He further elaborated the sharing of financial resources and work-load sharing between the Block Panchayats and Gram Panchayats. The entire discussion was made interactive as on most of the occasions the participants posited questions on each and every aspect explained by the president. The question and answer session cleared all the doubts about structure, function and performance of the institutions. The Gram Panchayat presidents of Tamil Nadu asked more number of questions on the participation and contribution of the people in the activities of the local bodies. The Block Panchayat President clearly explained how people contribute in kind or cash or even manual labour for the activities. Most of the schemes are being shared by the people and the government. The linkage between the Block and Gram Panchayat has been explained. It seemed that the government have participated in the schemes of the people.

From the Block Panchayat office, the team moved over to Erattupetta Gram Panchayat and met the president Mr. Aleyar. He explained the functioning of the Gram Panchayats. Planning process, decision-making process and implementing the decided works by the people, conducting Gram Sabha meeting, financial management have been explained in detail. He explained in detail how people are mobilised and oriented for the new task of planning. He emphasised the fact that all the activities are people-centred and they are to be executed only by the beneficiaries by themselves and not by either the president or any contractor. He narrated how their activities are conducted in a transparent way. After listening to the President of Gram Panchayat, the team took half an hour to have their lunch in hotel.

Immediately after the lunch they proceeded to another Gram Panchayat namely Melakavu Gram Panchayat. This Panchayat was visited with purpose of comparing the activities of the rich Panchayat with the poor Panchayat in terms of resources. Melakavu Gram Panchayat is poor in terms of resources. Even in the poor Panchayats, a variety of activities have been carried with the support and contribution of the people. The president narrated how people are prepared to contribute land, timbers and other material for creation of assets and facilities for the people. He also explained that management of financial resource is not a problem because they are getting maximum support from the people. It is interesting to note that even in the poor Panchayat, as per their estimate most of the basic facilities would be completed within eighteen months. The presidents said that Kerala Panchayats have been moving towards the unreached. After the discussion with Gram Panchayat presidents and vice-presidents, the team visited a few projects carried out by the beneficiaries themselves. The housing, road and drinking water well and a few other schemes have drawn the attention of all as they are being carried out by the people as beneficiaries. From there the team visited Ward-I Gram Sabha meeting in Erattupetta Panchayat. It was an eye-opener for many. The ward member Mrs. Shrine Nashrap was a Muslim woman migrated from Sri Lanka and settled in Kerala. She is vibrant and having the capacity to mobilise the women for public life through organising several self-help groups. Self-help group is her strength and it pulls crowds for Gram Sabha. Muslim women have come out of their houses for public life and they are organised at present. For all the self-help groups NABARD has given credit facilities. The team has seen the empowerment process of women while seeing the activities of the women in Ward-I of Erattupetta Panchayat.

After attending the Gram Sabha meeting, the team went to the lodge around 6.30 p.m. and they had a review of what they had perceived during their interaction with leaders and visits to schemes and programmes. The members indicated the following :

1. People have been centred for all their development activities.
2. People have come forward to help the Panchayats in all possible ways including mobilising resources for the activities of the Panchayats.
3. Self-help group has empowered the women.
4. Social development activities are the responsibilities of the people and not the government.
5. All activities are transparent and hence people trust the leaders.
6. Contractors have been replaced by the beneficiaries groups.
7. Planning has been done at the grassroot level.
8. More flexibility in operating the programmes and schemes.
9. While giving money to local bodies the government gives only broad guidelines and the rest lies with the Panchayats.
10. Gram Sabha is an activated and enlightened citizens body to control the Panchayats.
11. The leaders are capacitated leaders and they have vision about their village.
12. Politics does not disturb the development process in local bodies as in Tamil Nadu.
13. People perceive local bodies are development institutions and

not political institutions.

14. Panchayat leaders are full-time servants of the people.
15. The backbone of the bureaucracy has been broken and hence they are cooperating with the leaders.
16. Corruption prevails at a lower scale and among the officials.
17. The leaders are well paid commensurate with their responsibilities and workload.
18. Every Gram Panchayat has its own perspective vision report called development report.

Second day the team proceeded to Poonjar Thekkekara Gram Panchayat and had a lengthy discussion with the president. The president Mrs. Minerva Mohan explained in detail how she is performing her rôle as president. Especially women presidents from Tamil Nadu posited a large number of questions and Mrs. Minerva Mohan replied to all the questions to the satisfaction of the members of the team. Here, it is very important to note that women are empowered in Kerala even before the commencement of the New Panchayati Raj System. Women have no problem because of their gender. They have no fear in managing the public institutions. After their interaction with the president the team proceeded to a place where a Gram Sabha was scheduled to be held around 11 O'clock. The Gram Sabha meeting was organised in a school and attended by nearly three hundred members where the budget was presented and got the approval of the members of Gram Sabha. Discussions were held and questions were asked and both the president and the ward member replied to the queries of the members. The whole discussion centred round the role of self-help group in executing many programmes and schemes for the beneficiaries and for the general public. In the Gram Sabha meeting people expressed their views and grievances freely and one could notice the opportunity provided to the last man in the society to participate in the process of governance. After the meeting the team had discussion with the Gram Sabha members in groups. The members of the Gram Sabha have expressed the view that it is the Gram Sabha of the people and it is being convened by the president in accordance with the convenience of the people. The people had an opportunity to express their grievances and it is a place where social audit is being conducted.

From the Gram Sabha meeting the team went to the hotel for lunch and after the lunch they proceeded to the Block Panchayat Office for the review and to meet the press. The programme concluded with a resolution adopted by the leaders of the local bodies that they would strive to mobilise the people to achieve social development. They want to have holistic plan document as the development report of Kerala Panchayats Development report is a vision document of the people. The Gram Panchayat presidents want to have such documents in the printed form for their Panchayats also. They have indicated a number of works to be carried out in their Panchayats even without the assistance of the government. Likewise, the animators have also resolved to work in concert with Panchayat presidents to achieve the avowed objectives. The following works have been indicated :

1. Organising, self-help groups for women.
2. Conducting medical checkup for the people.
3. Awareness could be created among the people about the pre- and post-natal care, family welfare, child development and women development.
4. Eliminating dropouts in the schools.
5. Ensuring the entitlements to the people.
6. Making the villages green by planting saplings.
7. For all the activities wherever needed, people's contribution could be ensured.

After the resolution the Gram Panchayat presidents from Tamil Nadu briefed the press about their visits and indicated the initiatives which are going to be taken by them after their return to their respective Panchayats. They made a few clear-cut observations :

1. Their mindset has been changed. So far they acted as contractors for government and now they want to become the leaders of the people.
2. They have learnt the art of mobilising the people for development activities and to mobilise resources locally only after visiting the Panchayats and interacting with Kerala Panchayat presidents.
3. They have learnt how to organise self-help groups and how to establish linkage between the self-help group and the NABARD. The self-help group has acted as strong beneficiary group. This is an eye-opener for them.
4. To maintain sanitation and water supply in the rural areas, the available schemes and programmes of the government could be utilised.

The team finally expressed their sincere thanks to the presidents of Panchayats and Block Panchayat of Erattupetta for their valuable assistance and help in changing the mindset of the leaders of Gram Panchayats of Tamil Nadu. Further, it expressed its thanks to the Staff and Director of the Centre for Rural Management, Kottayam for their excellent arrangement for this programme. More specifically, the Gram Panchayat presidents passed a resolution recording their gratefulness to the Population Foundation of India for its earnest interest in grassroot democracy by facilitating them to visit Kerala Panchayat, and to acquaint themselves in the Kerala model of development. The programme came to an end with a deep meditation on what they are going to do in their panchayats.

**Details of Training and Number of Local Body Leaders Trained**

| Sl. No. | Institution sponsored | No. of leaders trained | Remarks |
|---|---|---|---|
| 1. | Tamil Nadu Institute of Urban Studies | 2150 | Town Panchayats Municipalities and Women Leaders |
| 2. | CAPART | 599 | Village Panchayat Presidents |
| 3. | WS DANIDA | 808 | Village Panchayat Presidents and Vice-Presidents |
| 4. | Population Foundation of India | 1278 | Panchayat Panchayat Union District Panchayat |
| 5. | Tamil Nadu Social Welfare Board | 500 | Women Presidents of Village Panchayats |
| 6. | NGOs/NYKs | 400 | Members and Presidents of Rural/ Urban Local Bodies |

*Source* : Computed.

# 8

# TRAINING PROGRAMME CONDUCTED FOR GRAM PANCHAYAT WOMEN PRESIDENTS OF MADURAI, RAMANATHAPURAM AND PUDUKKOTTAI DISTRICTS*

## Perception of the Leaders on New Panchayati Raj System

Before the commencement of the training exercise a schedule is being circulated among the trainees to elicit their perception and understanding of the New Panchayati Raj System. Their perceptions are explained here.

The perception that Panchayats are to perform the service functions is linkering in the minds of leaders as they are not aware of the provisions and main implications of the New Panchayati Raj System. They had a rough idea about the new system that it would fulfil the basic needs of the people and provide basic amenities to the community. They presumed that more powers would be given to Panchayats and equally more amount of money would also be given to Panchayats. This has been created among the people by the media. They said that they did not find copies of the 73rd amendment to the Constitution of India and hence they did not read the provisions of the act. They did not care to read the provisions of the Tamil Nadu Panchayati Act 1994, even though it was supplied to the Gram Panchayat leaders as the entire act is in a language which is not understandable to them despite that it is in Tamil. Even the candidates who have contested in the election have not gone through the act when it was enacted. Likewise they had a notion that the political parties will not evince keen interest in conducting the election. The moment election was

* Sponsored by CAPART, Hyderabad.

announced, they contested in the fray with the hope to enjoy more powers and resources as MPs and MLAs. They have openly admitted that they have spent money for electioneering between rupees thirty five thousand to two lakhs.

In the interview schedule which was administered to elicit the opinion of the leaders, there are about twelve questions. They are :

(a) basic objectives of the new Panchayati Raj system;
(b) special features of the new system;
(c) functions of the new Panchayati Raj system;
(d) responsibilities of the presidents of Gram Panchayat;
(e) ways and means to perform their role successfully;
(f) methodology of organising the people and to involve them in the development activities of the community.
(g) possibilities for rural economic development;
(h) people's participation in Panchayat activities;
(i) women's development;
(j) SC/ST development activities;
(k) Social justice, and
(1) the characteristics of a good leader in the panchayat.

Their responses to the above questions are as follows :

(a) Panchayat is to elicit their basic needs;
(b) Panchayat is to fulfil the basic needs;
(c) Panchayat is to implement the Government schemes for the poor.
(d) Panchayat is to provide basic facilities in the rural areas;
(e) Panchayat has three tier panchayat system
(f) Panchayat will be a permanent entity;
(g) Panchayat will have 29 subjects in 11th schedule;
(h) Panchayat will have a Gram Sabha;
(i) Panchayat is to select beneficiaries for government schemes;
(j) Panchayat is to supervise fair price shop;
(k) Panchayat is to mobilise resources for Panchayats;
(l) Panchayat is to construct culverts, bridges, houses for the poor;
(m) Panchayat is to lay roads, and dig wells;
(n) Panchayat is to maintain sanitation;
(o) Panchayat is to protect the environment;
(p) Panchayat is to do afforestation activities;
(q) Panchayat is to protect the common property resources;
(r) Panchayat is to take steps to women's development;

(s) Panchayat is to convene the Panchayat meetings periodically; and
(t) panchayat is to organise Gram Sabha meeting periodically.

The presidents of Gram Panchayats are having a rough idea about what the Panchayats can do and again reiterate the service functions as the functions of the Panchayats. They forget about the original functions of the local bodies as per the provisions of the act. They are not well aware of the basic objective of the 73rd Constitutional amendment. They have not mentioned about the economic development activities and social justice. Because of the past three years, the Gram Panchayat leaders are oriented only in implementing the schemes and programmes of the governments. Even in discussion they ask more questions about schemes. They are not much worried about the planning and resource mobilization for economic activities.

**Problems the Women Leaders have faced in the field**

Group discussions are being arranged to elicit their problems face in the field while performing their role and functions. Their problems are presented here.

1. Presidents of Gram Panchayats are not aware of all the rural development programmes and schemes. They know only a few programmes from the officials. Even for a few schemes they are not able to get the full details from the officials.
2. Needs of the people are going on increasing which need enormous amount of resources. To meet all their requirements there is no comprehensive plan and moreover they have no adequate resources.
3. Employees and teachers working in the purview of Panchayats, are not employees of the Panchayats and they are all employees of the Government and hence the employees are not accountable to local bodies; as a result schools are not properly managed. Yet the presidents are made accountable to the people for the proper functioning of the schools in the villages.
4. Resources (both in the form of money mobilised from within and drawn from Panchayat union and DRDA for schemes) are inadequate to meet the demands;
5. Capacity of the workers working in the rural areas are inadequate to meet the problems in the rural society. Attending the repair

works in the street light or motors fixed in overhead tanks is not in time and the technicians caused inordinate delay. Rates for the repairing work is very low and hence nobody turns towards these works. For the purchase of materials for the repairing works or replacement, presidents have no option but to give more money than the market rate and where they will go for this extra payment. Naturally they will indulge in corrupt practice. Even if they want to be honest the system would not permit them to be honest.

6. Providing shelter is a major problem in the rural areas. Whether it is providing *patta* or getting housing scheme presidents have to face hell of problems as needs are more and available resources are limited. Moreover, while providing these facilities discretion of officials plays an important role rather than the procedures of the programmes and schemes.
7. IRDP beneficiary selection is a major problem due to the interference of the politicians, MLAs and MPs.
8. Getting the village map is very difficult from the revenue officials because large number of irregularities have been committed by the revenue officials in the matter of common properties. Absolutely there is no cooperation from the revenue department and other sectoral departments in this regard.
9. It is very difficult to remove encroachment from the common properties. It requires the support of Revenue Department and Police. As per the government order they have to support the Panchayat to remove all encroachments of the common properties. It is unfortunate that officials are cooperating with the Panchayats for eviction.
10. Common property resources have not been maintained well to yield income to Panchayats since they are not under the control of the local bodies. They are being encroached by influencing individuals.
11. Needs are unmet even after the panchayats came into being.
12. No relationship between the needs and the schemes.
13. Still we have complicated administrative procedures at the lower level.
14. Difficult to provide employment opportunities to the needy.
15. Officials domination over the elected leaders is evident and they dictate terms to the leaders.
16. People's mind-set is that everything has to be done by the government. People are only to receive. They expect each and

everything to be taken care of by the local body leaders.

17. Common property resource management should be given to local bodies. Sand, quary and other natural resources are the properties of the community. But now on a single order they are taken away from the people without getting the consent of the community.
18. Powers of the Union Engineer (UE) are unlimited and UE is the embodiment of corruption. He is more powerful than the Block Development Officer. He is the person responsible for clearing bills, proposals and hence he makes the Gram Panchayat presidents to dance to his tune. Union Engineer demands 15 per cent commission for each and every work.
19. Interference of MPs and MLAs in the affairs of local bodies is more and their words are respected and their interference in the local body affairs disturb the activities of the local bodies. Increasing the amount for MLAs and MPs would attempt to kill the local bodies.
20. In all government functions organised in the rural areas, the concerned constituency MP and MLA are invited but the local body leaders are not respected and invited.
21. Presidents are elected by the people and Vice-presidents of Gram Panchayats are elected by ward members. But to sign the cheque, it was made that Vice-president should also sign. It disturbs the atmosphere and administration. Vice-presidents demand money to put his or her signature.
22. Women presidents are not respected by the officials. Sometimes they were illtreated in the offices. They face lot of problems in the offices of the government.
23. More fiexibility should be given in the schemes to local body leaders to meet the basic needs of the people.
24. Public distribution system should be supervised by the panchayats in the local areas.
25. Government orders are not properly circulated among the local body leaders.
26. For each and every transaction officials in the Panchayat union demand money openly.
27. There is no linkage between Panchayat and the cooperatives.
28. Makkal Nala Paniyalargal are in the Panchayats and they have to work under Panchayats and they have to get their salary from Panchayats. Yet, in practice they are not working in coordination with the president. Hence the procedure of giving salary to them

in Panchayat union office should be stopped. Now only government have raised and they are brought under the control of the Gram Panchayats.

29. Ration cards are to be distributed through Gram Sabha to elimate bogus cards.
30. For making estimate and settlement of bills, officials take lot of time but to execute the programmes and schemes officials give very short duration to the leaders. This has to be avoided.
31. Birth certificate, Death certificate, Community certificate should be issued by the Panchayats through resolution. Erring leaders have to be punished. Now these certificates are being given by the officials (revenue) after getting Rs. 300 as bribe.
32. There is no linkage between the revenue department and the development departments.
33. The role of District Panchayat is not known to Gram Panchayat presidents.
34. MPs, MLAs, District Panchayat Members, Block Panchayat Members are operating funds to execute certain works in the villages without the knowledge of the people and the Gram Panchayats. All these works are to be integrated. Now these works were not on the basis of need and hence lot of money is being wasted by allotting them for construction work.
35. Panchayats are advised to take up works without claiming any advance. Where do they find money for work? Even after completing the work the presidents have to move from pillar to post to get their money from the offices and for which they have to give bribe to officials at all levels.
36. Allocation of money to MP, MLA, District Panchayat Member, Block Panchayat Member tempted the Village Panchayat Ward Members to pose that they should also be given some amount of money for works.

**Input given by the Resource Persons**

1. Background of 73rd Constitutional Amendment.
2. Salient features of 73rd Constitutional Amendment.
3. Features of the Panchayati Act of Tamil Nadu 1994.
4. Powers and responsibilities entrusted to Panchayats.
5. Government orders passed in Tamil Nadu akin to Panchayats.
6. Schemes and programmes of both governments.

7. Water supply and sanitation.
8. Pre-natal and post-natal care.
9. Children and women development.
10. Multi Level Planning in PRI's.
11. Employment Generation and administering social justice.
12. Agriculture and Animal Husbandry.
13. Common Property Resource Management.
14. Maintenance of Accounts.
15. Resource Mobilisation.
16. Participatory Planning.
17. Self Help Groups and Village Industries.
18. Participatory Governance through Gram Sabha.
19. Environmental issues.
20. Communication skill.
21. Improving Leadership qualities.
22. Transparency and accountability.
23. People's charter and its implication.
24. Making this institution as people's institutions.
25. Containing corruption at the Grassroots level.
26. Gender sensitization.
27. Special focus on (SGSY).

**People's Expectations as perceived by the Leaders**

1. Approach road to the burial ground belonging to SC community and BC community.
2. Upgradation of metal road into Block Toproad.
3. Additional building for PDS due to more family cards.
4. Veterinary sub-centre.
5. Group Housing Scheme.
6. Hand pumps.
7. Replacing the Iron Post (street lights) with cement post as the EB wireman refuses to climb over the iron post.
8. Approach roads to helmet villages.
9. Removal of encroachments of road and street leading to SC habitation.
10. Increasing the number of lineman (EB) according to the number of street lights.
11. Overhead Tank.
12. TWARD board incomplete works must be completed.

13. More trips of buses to their villages.
14. Plan for improving and maintaining Common Property Resources.
15. To provide Sanitation facilities during festival time sanctioned amount is not sufficient.
16. Employment opportunities to young men and women.
17. Repair work at overhead tanks.

**Leaders Perception after the Training**

Before the Valedictory session, again an interview schedule is being distributed to elicit their opinion about the implications of training. Apart from filling up the schedule, they openly express their opinion about the training programme in the Valedictory session. Some VIP will be there in each programme to distribute the certificate. The session has an advantage for the trainers to correct themselves in their methodology of the training. Their perceptions about the Panchayati Raj after the training programme have been compiled and presented below.

1. They perceived the long-term implications of the new Panchayati Raj System.
2. The mind-set that local bodies are to execute schemes and programmes of the governments has been changed and the new mind set that local bodies are to work for economic development and social justice has been created.
3. They learnt to make the Panchayats as people's Panchayats and not the government's Panchayats.
4. It is not power but it is only responsibility that makes the Panchayats as self governing institution.
5. They realise that without money Panchayats can do many programmes in the villages.
6. They realise the original functions of the local bodies.
7. They feel that they are change agents.
8. Key provisions of the 73rd Constitutional Amendment Act and Tamil Nadu Panchayati Raj Act are known to the Gram Panchayat presidents.
9. How to prepare perspective plan for rural development? is known to them.
10. It is recognised as a governing institution.
11. Schemes and programmes of the government are known to them.
12. Role and responsibilities of the presidents are known to them.

13. How to create employment opportunities in the villages by making use of the available skills? is known to them.
14. How to mobilize resources in the rural areas? is known to them.
15. How to make the Panchayats as movement of the people? is known to them.
16. How to get the government orders from the officials? is known to them.
17. How to get the works done in the government offices? is known to them.
18. How to conduct the Panchayat administration in a transparent way? is known to them.
19. How to mobilize people and to involve them in the Panchayat activities? are known to them.
20. Issues and solutions are known to them.
21. How to protect the environment? is known to them.
22. How to make the rural areas Green? is known to them.

**Points Aggregated from the Group Discussion**

***Madurai District***

1. Political interference and politisation of issues by party men in the villages. They look at Panchayats as political institutions and not as development institutions.
2. The people are not at all satisfied with the necessary facilities provided to them. Their demands are always on the increase in geometrical proportion.
3. Selection of beneficiaries is not an easy job. Every political segment wants to include the names of its candidates in the beneficiary list. Hence the final selection is done by the officials. People have been oriented to obey the officials and not to the leaders. Still people have hopes in the officials.
4. The community control over the society is more than the Panchayat control where one community is large in number. Still community Panchayats are powerful.
5. The ward members demanded that their ward must be given in priority in all the works. Everyone wants to please the people by hook or by crook.
6. The allocation of fund is not proportionate to total population. Wherever SC and ST population is more, fund allocations are

abundant. But the conditions of the caste Hindus hamlets are also on par with the hamlets of the SC and ST. In several villages the variation of the total population is more than 2000. Our administration acts on wrong data base.

7. The Hand Pump are not functioning well. The depth of water table has gone down very deeply.
8. The House tax may be increased. But people resist and further party men are instigating the people to resist it. People are willing but politicians are instigating the people not to give.
9. The PHC supposed to be functioning round the clock are not functioning till night. Hence poor people sought Panchayats president's support to take the patients to towns for treatment.
10. There must be a special meeting of all representatives to discuss and decide the various developmental activities of the villages and the possible ways and means to augment resources for the same from within and from the State and Central Governments. This initiative has to be taken by the inspector of Panchayats. Inspector of Panchayats should have a facilitating role in the Panchayati system rather than inspecting role. At present the Inspector of Panchayat has come to take action only against the president of the Gram Panchayats.
11. The officials released the fund not in time but they chase the president to complete the work quickly. Hence quality is not ensured. It seems that the schemes are to spend money and not to ensure facility to the people.
12. Sufficient awareness must be created among the people on the significance of Gram Sabha. In the absence of awareness, Gram Sabha is a grievance redressal sabha.
13. Anna Marumalarchi Thittam — the selection process is not transparent. The MLAs are expecting commission to select the Panchayat. Hence only poor Panchayat should be selected for AMT as per the norms.
14. The village commons should be entrusted to the Panchayat. But now they are with traditional Panchayats and some of them are with influential individuals. We can control and check the encroachments by entrusting the power and responsibility to Panchayats. Further the commons could be enriched and fruitfully utilised. There is a lot of scope for augment resources from the common properties.
15. The government officials especially the field level officials must

be asked to stay in the villages. Workers and officials of rural development are not living in the villages. They are also conducting rural development tourism.

16. The police administration is not helpful in dealing with encroachment problem. Eventhough the government order clearly states that the police have to help the panchayats in this regard, the police are always in the hands of the vested interests.
17. The revenue officials are not seriously functioning to protect common property resources. They even allow the individuals to encroach public way to burial ground.
18. At least once in two months the district authorities must meet presidents.
19. MP/ MLA fund allocation has to be abrogated or atleast streamlined otherwise a huge amount of money is going to be wasted. MLA's and MPs are doing some work which are not the felt needs of the people.
20. Even to receive ration card, we have to mobilise people and take public action like *dharna*. This type of indifferent attitude has to be checked on the part of the officials.
21. The irregularities in PDS should be dealt with seriously by the officials or it can be brought under the control of Panchayats. People are bringing complaints only to the presidents. For the effective functioning of PDS Central Government believes the Panchayats can do it better and the State Government believes the officials can do better.
22. The ex-presidents and defeated candidates create problems on most of the occasions in the Panchayat administration. Instead of cooperation, they always develop conflict with Panchayat Council.
23. The grievance reddressal system is very complicated and expensive. For example, when the caste Hindu encroached the land site earmarked for SC community housing, the problem is not sorted out by the officials. The president took the case to the court and redeem the land after a struggle. It takes money, energy and time.
24. The works undertaken in the villages by other tiers of Panchayats are not known to the village Panchayats and people are not consulted whether that work is needed or not.
25. Training is very essential for Panchayat leaders for their effective functioning. But the Government of Tamil Nadu has not given

serious attention to the training aspect. Now atleast Gandhigram Rural Institute is giving such training. It should not be an one time affair. It should be a continuous one.

26. The help and support of family male members is needed due to the villagers non-cooperation and groupism.
27. Uneducated and uninterested women presidents only allow their husbands/male members of their family to interfere in the administration of the Panchayat and others only seek support and help from the male members of their family. It should not be treated as proxy. It will be proxy only when the space of the women is operated by men or others.
28. The house tap connections permitted during the official tenure have to be disconnected now. When the presidents take necessary steps towards this decision, the officials are not supporting the presidents for their actions. Most of the occasions the officials are creating problems in the villages.
29. To replace the street lights the E.B. staff demand more money than what is permitted.
30. The existing procedure for repairing electric motors is illogical one. For the whole district two to three persons are given licence whereas a large number of motors have to be repaired immediately. In each block, there must be one or two motor mechanics, approved by government.
31. The vacancy of positions in village schools should be filled up immediately.
32. The schools are not clean and the environment is not so conducive for learning. We have no control over school administration. We have to maintain only school building. It is illogical on the part of the government to give building to Panchayats and retaining the staff with them.
33. The government appointed Makkal Nala Paniyalarkal are not useful to Panchayats. They obey their pay master in union. They are party men doing party work at the cost of the people. Sometimes they are anti-social elements.
34. The G.O. and other guidelines pertaining to local administration are not properly sent to the Panchayats.
35. There must be a special fund to improve the poor Panchayats.

***Ramanathapuram District***

36. The relationship between the presidents and the officials are

smooth because of the intervention of the Inspector of Panchayats. But it is not a permanent feature.

37. Due to power fluctuation, the street lighting is always a problem, and hence people are bringing complaints and they are not attended to by the EB staff responsively.
38. We are able to provide tanks, library, drinking water, school building, PDS building shelter to passengers and street lights in the villages. But people expect further facilities such as House tap connection, drainage, cement pavement in the street and sweeper services which demands more finance.
39. We are able to obtain land for overhead tank and PDS shop. It could not be possible during the officials tenure. Yet our achievements are not recognised.
40. Involving community leadership is a technique for smooth functioning and to avoid conflict between official Panchayats and traditional Panchayats.
41. With the help of women *sangams* we are doing *shramdan* works. But while the noon-meal scheme implementation was evaluated, the *sangam* of noon meal workers threatened the president. In this situation people have not come forward to help the presidents.
42. The Block level monitoring committee for noon meal scheme appointed by the government is not properly functioning due to its limited membership in the committee.
43. There are still a few villages where there is no drinking water facility. The TWAD scheme is not yet reached there.
44. We have involved ourselves in school activities and we have encouraged sports and cultural events for children in the schools. We collected public fund for upgrading middle school to high school. Even without adequate powers, we are doing our best to provide quality education to our people.
45. The people living in the extension area are expecting all facilities for them in one stroke which is highly impossible at present.
46. We maintain the communal harmony in the villages but the political parties are working in a different style and they are creating clashes among the caste groups.
47. We formed approach road to the remote villages through Namakku Name Thittam.
48. We spent money for improving the bank of the irrigation tanks and we are not able to maintain the same due to the interference of the officials.

49. There are villages where electricity service is not yet reached.
50. The officials are not giving special attention to the buildings of Balwadi/School which need immediate repair work and we find usual delay in this also.

***Pudukottai District***

51. Unaware of the details of fund allocation under various schemes in the various departments of the government.
52. Lack of knowledge and practice in augmenting more resources to improve the financial position of the Panchayat.
53. The other two tiers have no link with Gram Panchayats.
54. The MLA, MP area development allocation is not reaching the non-party presidents for their activities in the rural areas.
55. Non-implementation of the resolutions passed in the Gram Sabha meetings resulted in non-cooperation of people to the Panchayats.
56. No records available about Common Property Resources in the villages.
57. Officials have helped the influential individuals to encroach the common properties.
58. The auction of social forestry trees is unduly delayed in spite of repeated requests. The revenue officials are indifferent in this assignment.
59. The fishery right is vested with the private party in a village tank. The domination of caste Panchayat over the common is a very big problem in the villages.
60. No special grant for maintenance of CPR. Over 40 years, poor are residing over the sides of the tankbund. But *patta* is not issuing to them.
61. Poor families in Backward Community are also demanding group housing facility.

— The repair work at SC group house was not undertaken as promised by higher officials.
— The MLA, MP fund allocation mostly for their own party people.
— Untouchability is still persisting in rural areas. Revenue officials do not seriously attend to this problem. Police force is not coming to protect the SC.
— VAO, Police and Revenue officials are joining their hands to protect

the selfish interest of the encroachers.

— The agriculture engineering department, forest department, are not showing any interest in the Panchayats when they are implementing their schemes.

— The Gram Sabha attendance is in the diminishing trend due to non fulfilling of their earlier demands and expectations.

**Materials Supplied to Them**

1. A Printed Book of 400 pages with details of 73rd Constitutional Amendment Act

— With details of the Tamil Nadu Rural Local Body Act of 1994.

— With a brief history of Panchayati Raj.

— With a brief outline of Planning Experience in India.

— Micro Level Planning and participative development process.

— All schemes and programmes of the Centre and State governments with all details.

— Resource mobilization.

— Common Property Resource Management.

— Importance and implications of community action.

— MPs Area development programme details.

— MLAs constituency development programme details and the hurdles to make Panchayat as self governing institutions.

2. All government orders pertinent to Local Bodies.
3. A well designed jute bag.
4. A scribbling pad.
5. A Pen.
6. Important addresses of institutions to get more informations about Panchayat activities.
7. A charter of Panchayats.
8. A book on people's participation in Panchayat activities — Kerala Experiences.

**Conclusion**

The capacity building exercise for Gram Panchayat Presidents has to go a long way to achieve its results. It is a good beginning by which their mind-set has been changed. Lot of information have been exchanged. Their potentiality has been drawn out. 60 per cent of attendance has been ensured. Material supplied to them are properly used by the participants of the training programme. Women leaders have evinced keen interest in listening the lectures. One aspect is obvious from their interactions — i.e., they need a supporting base as government officials are not favourable to them. They feel that they are not properly oriented either by the officials or by the family members who are guiding them for their action. But in the slow process they have gained confidence. They said that their struggle is silent. In the silent struggle a section of the women leaders have come to a conclusion that they have to withdraw from this space. But there is a section with a good number of leaders who have determined to continue in the space created for them and they have identified the supportive organisations and through which they gain support and strength. One important aspect that the utilisation of the space created for women by the women has to be seriously looked into by our research endeavour.

# INDEX